Next Century Art

By *John Blandly*
Copyright © MMXXII by J.J. Brearton
AvantLifeGuard Books
All Rights Reserved
Imprimatur
Nihil Obstat

Part One
Twenty Second Century Art

Part Two
Art and Limericks
Art and Limericks

Part Three

Art eBook

Part One
Twenty Second Century Art

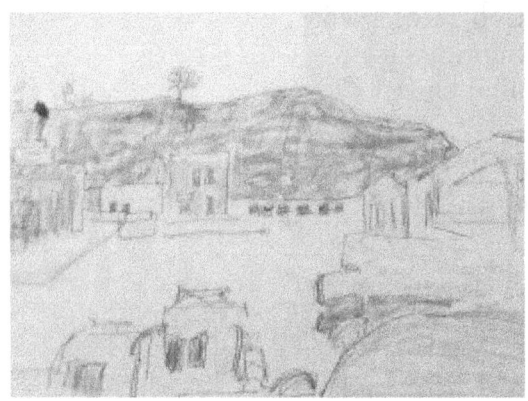

Mount Olympus, Troy, NY

Blandly likes to talk about himself in the third person. Caesar did this too. Of course, Caesar had far better adventures.

Blandly is hoping he doesn't end up like Caesar, who died when he was stabbed in the back 22 times on the steps of the Roman Forum.

Talk about overkill.

Another famous Roman, Cicero, was stabbed in the back while trying to cross a creek to escape assassins.

Emperors, like modern rock stars, rocketed to fame and glory and were quickly killed off.

The numerous paintings we refer to (here, Blandly's multiple personalities kick in), were often small, on newsprint, and reflected the scant time he felt he had left.

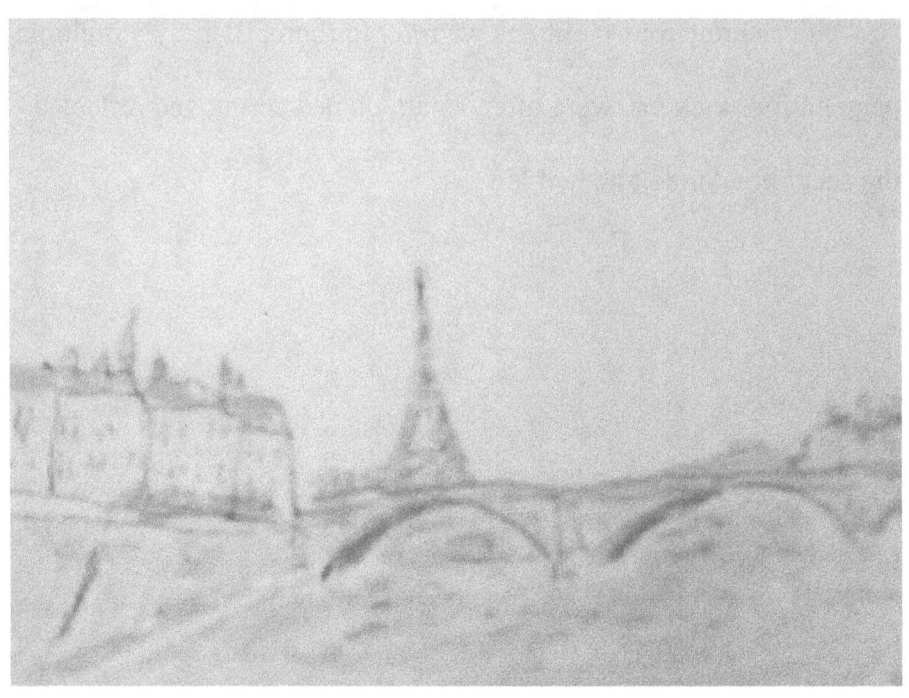

Blandly tried very hard to do a decent painting of the Eiffel Tower.

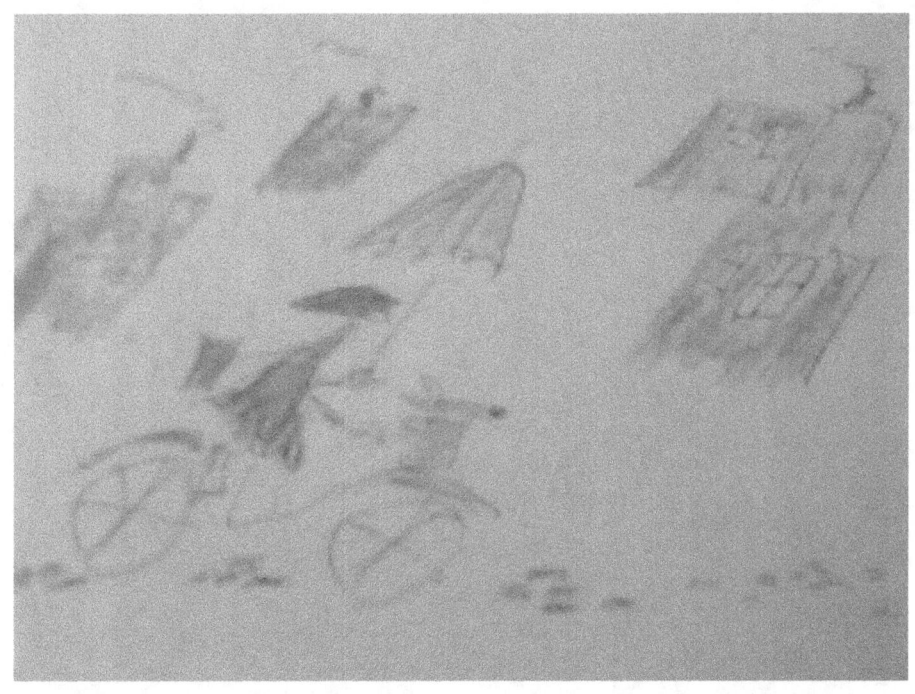

Some paintings were done after seeing French art on Twitter, like the above.

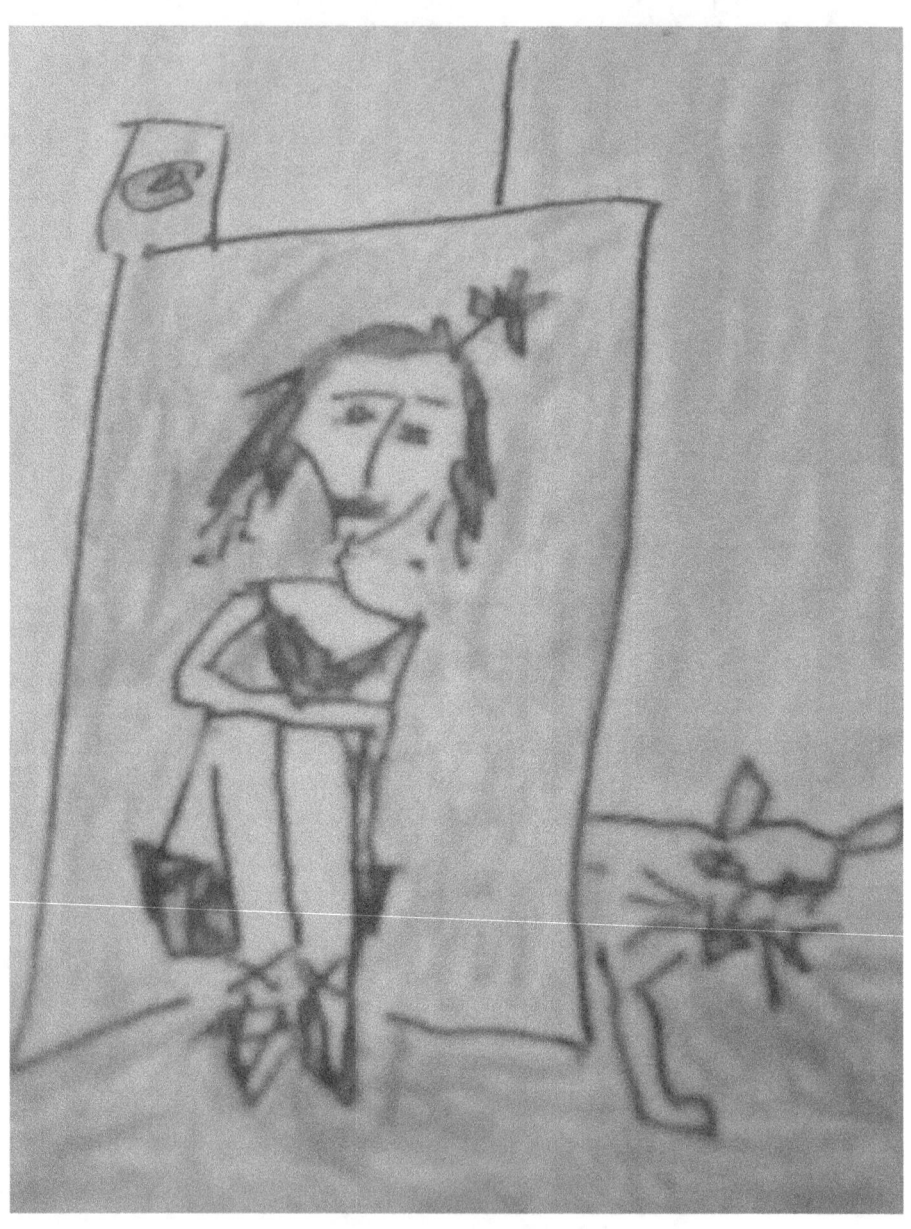

Blandly liked painting portraits of women, which he said was difficult. He reworked some almost endlessly.

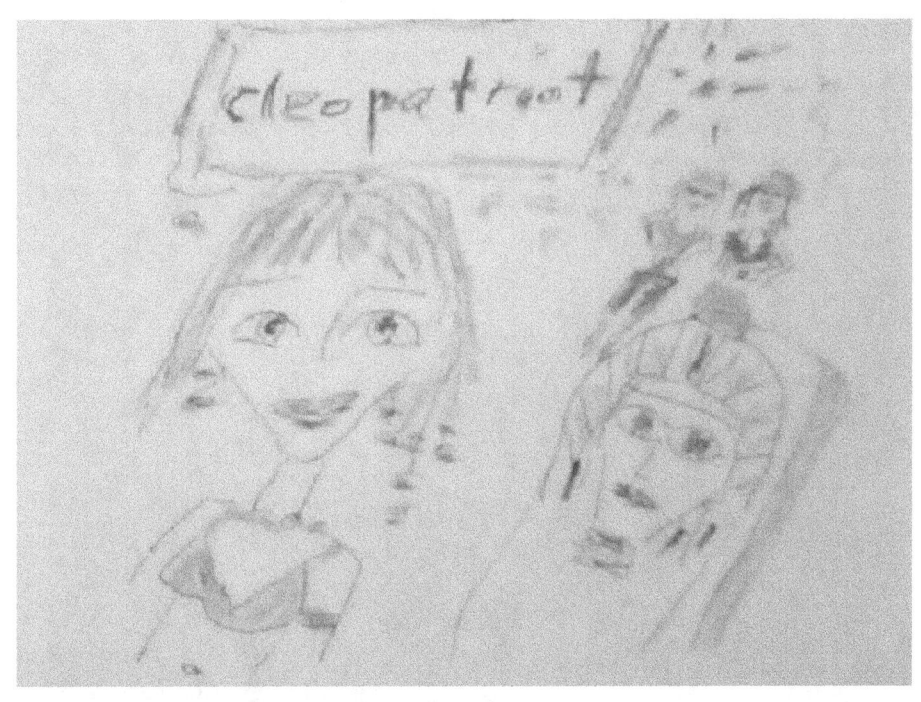

A painting Blandly saw online inspired "Cleo".

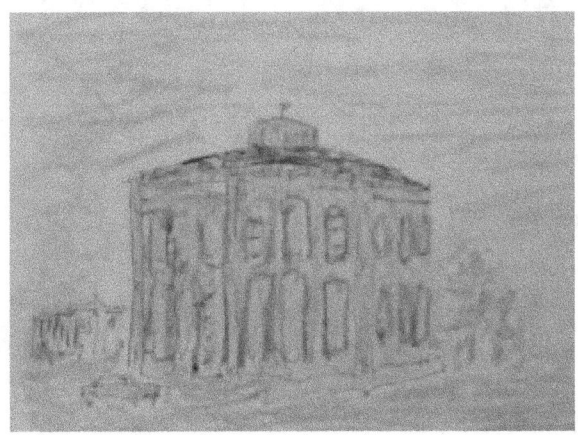

Gasholder House, Troy, NY

Spencertown Art Academy

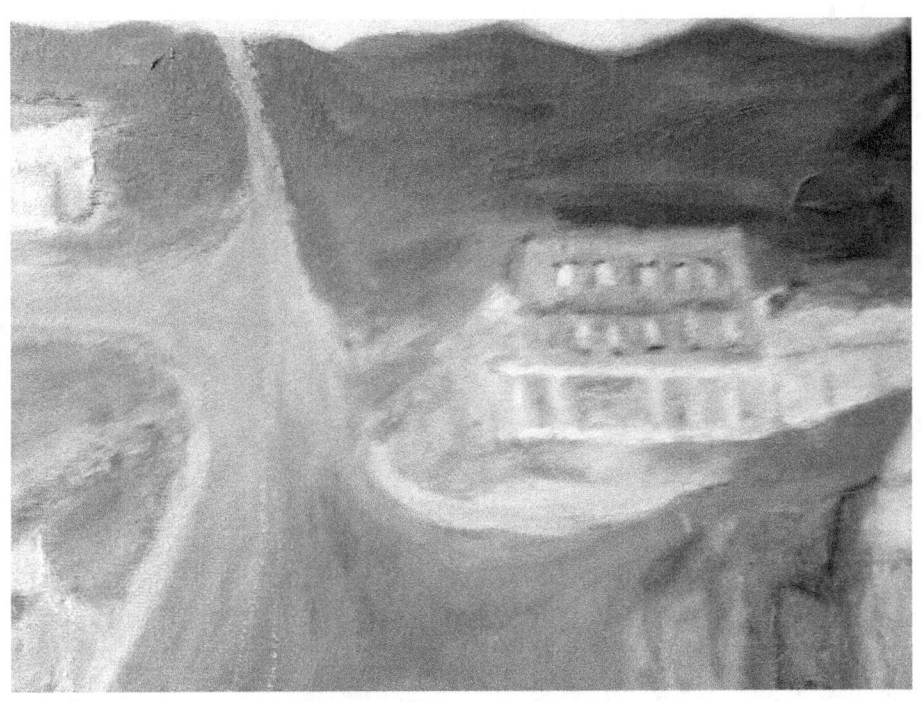

Vermont Bookstore--oil on canvas--12x9

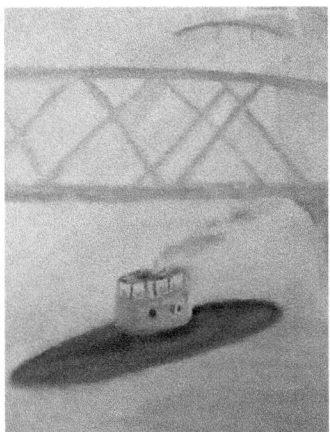

The monitor 18x14 oil on canvas

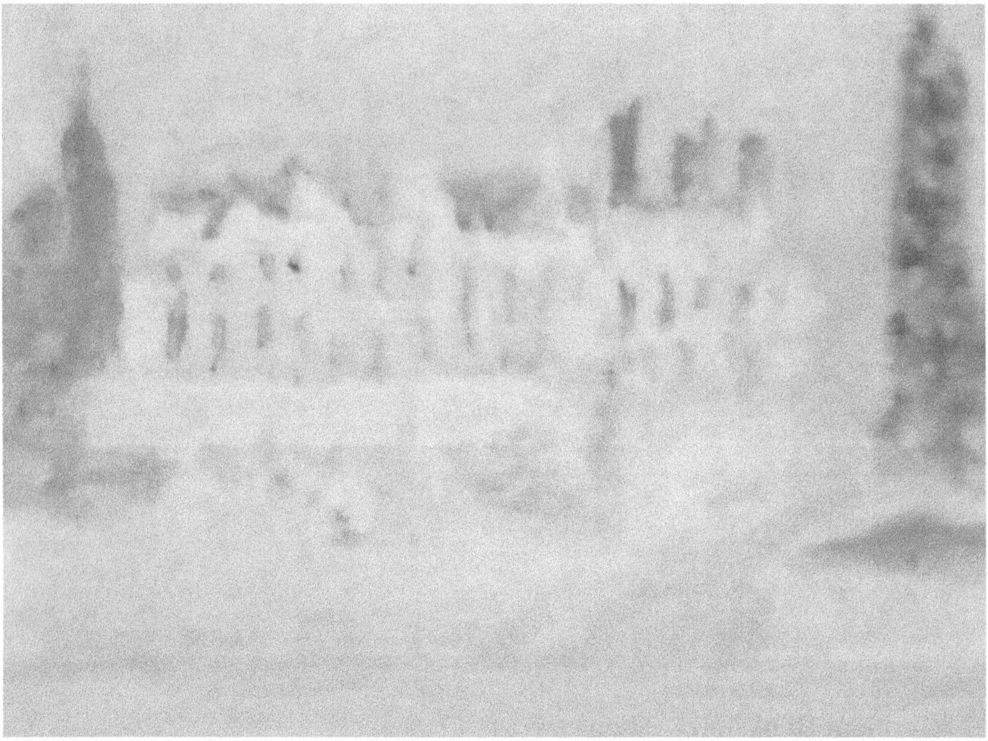

Red Lion in Winter--oil on canvas—12x9

Selections from, "Art eBook," by John Blandly

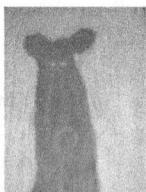

The Bear

Dimensions 1 ½' X 4 ½ '---a large oil painting on wood, "The Bear" appears on the back cover of the book, "The Greatest Novel Ever Written," as a photo of "the author."

Sold after an exhibition at the Spencertown Art Center, Spencertown, NY.

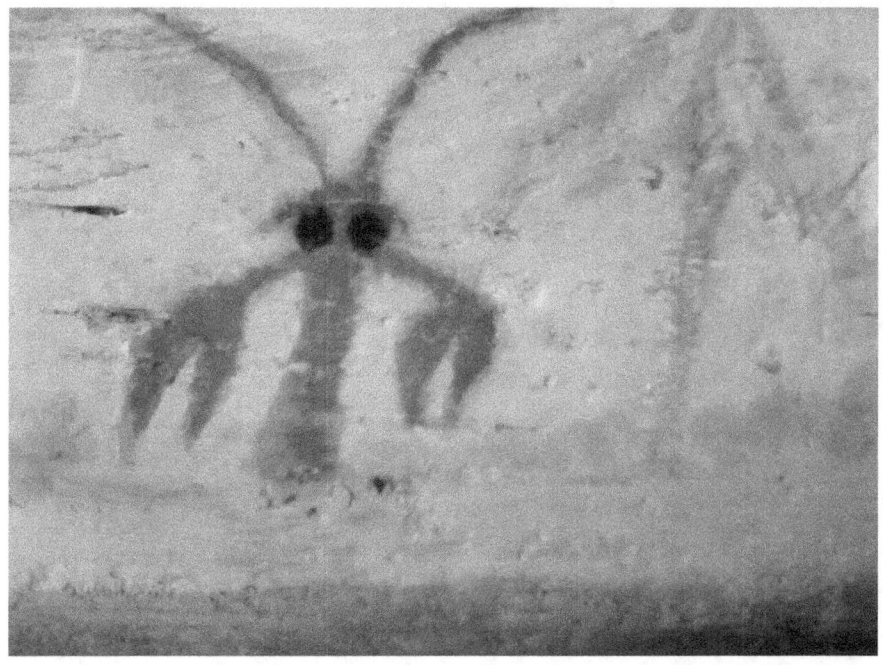

This painting, "Beach Lobster," was also sold at the Spencertown Art Center after an exhibition.

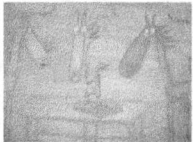

A very small photo of "Saratoga Writers Group." Blandly brought this painting to a session of his writers group and had a photo taken of the group behind the painting. He cannot locate the photo.

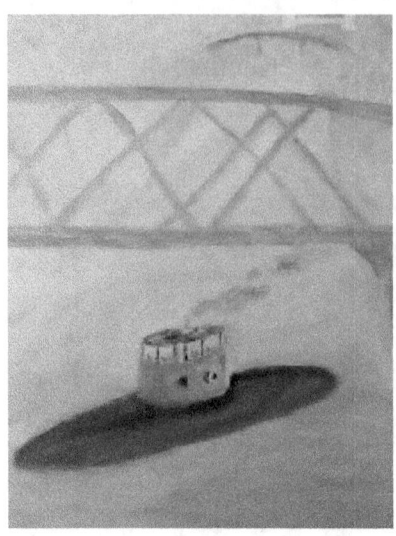

USS Monitor

Fairly accurate oil painting, on wood, of Blandly's exciting and fantastic hometown. He has used it on zazzle t-shits, the only product he has ever sold there.

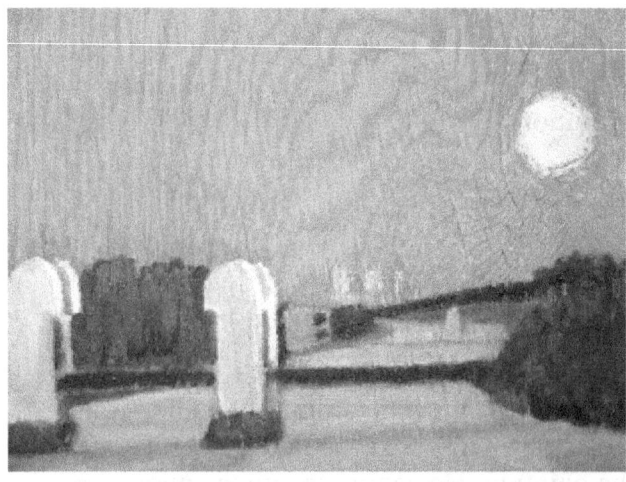

Troy

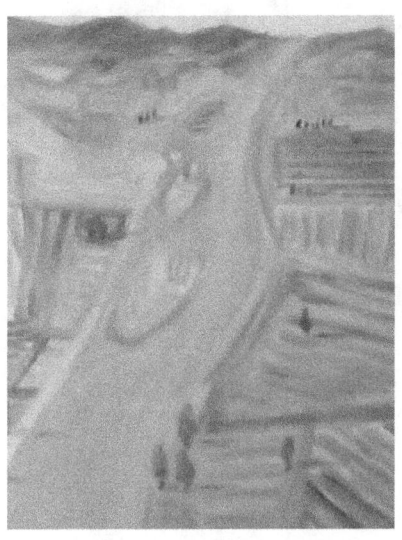

TroCoWaWaMeGi

A painting, Wayne Thiebald style, of the cities of Troy, Cohoes, Watervliet, Waterford, Menands, and Green Island, in upstate New York, a small metropolitan area with common interests, whose residents often attend the same high schools.

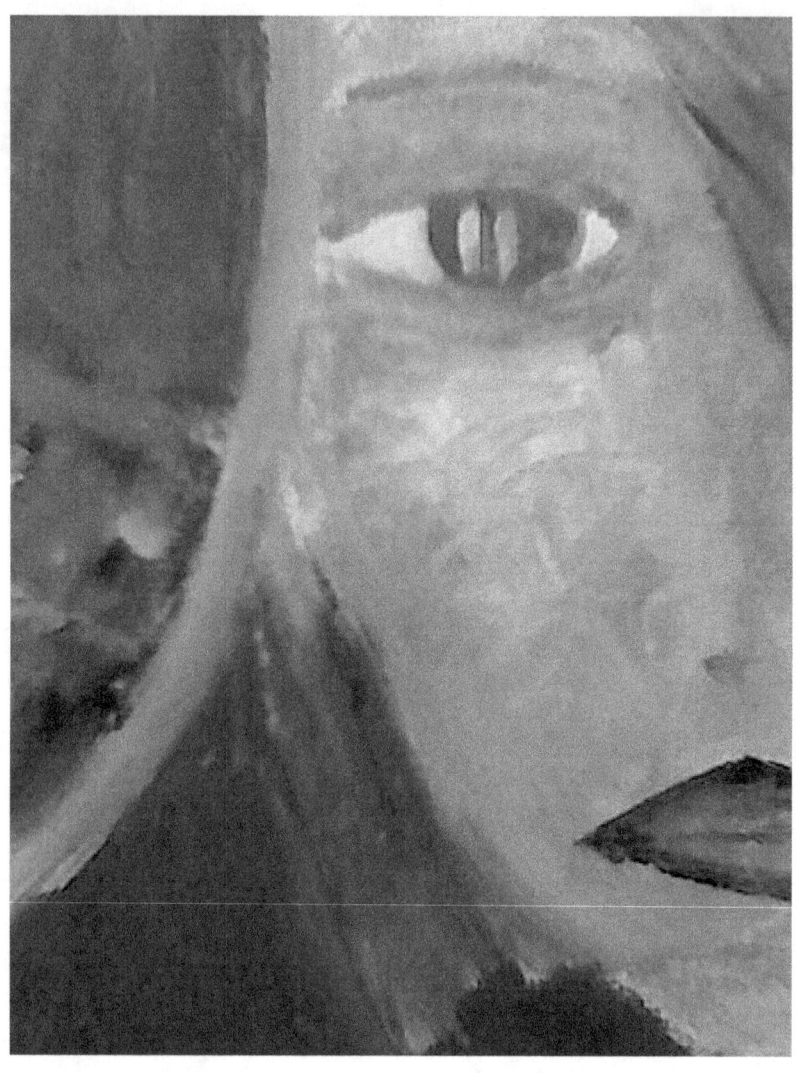

A small part of "Artgirl" based in part on a famous painting that depicts the World Trade Center Towers reflected in the girl's eye. The original painting was by Michael Perez, who painted a series of paintings he called "America the Beautiful."

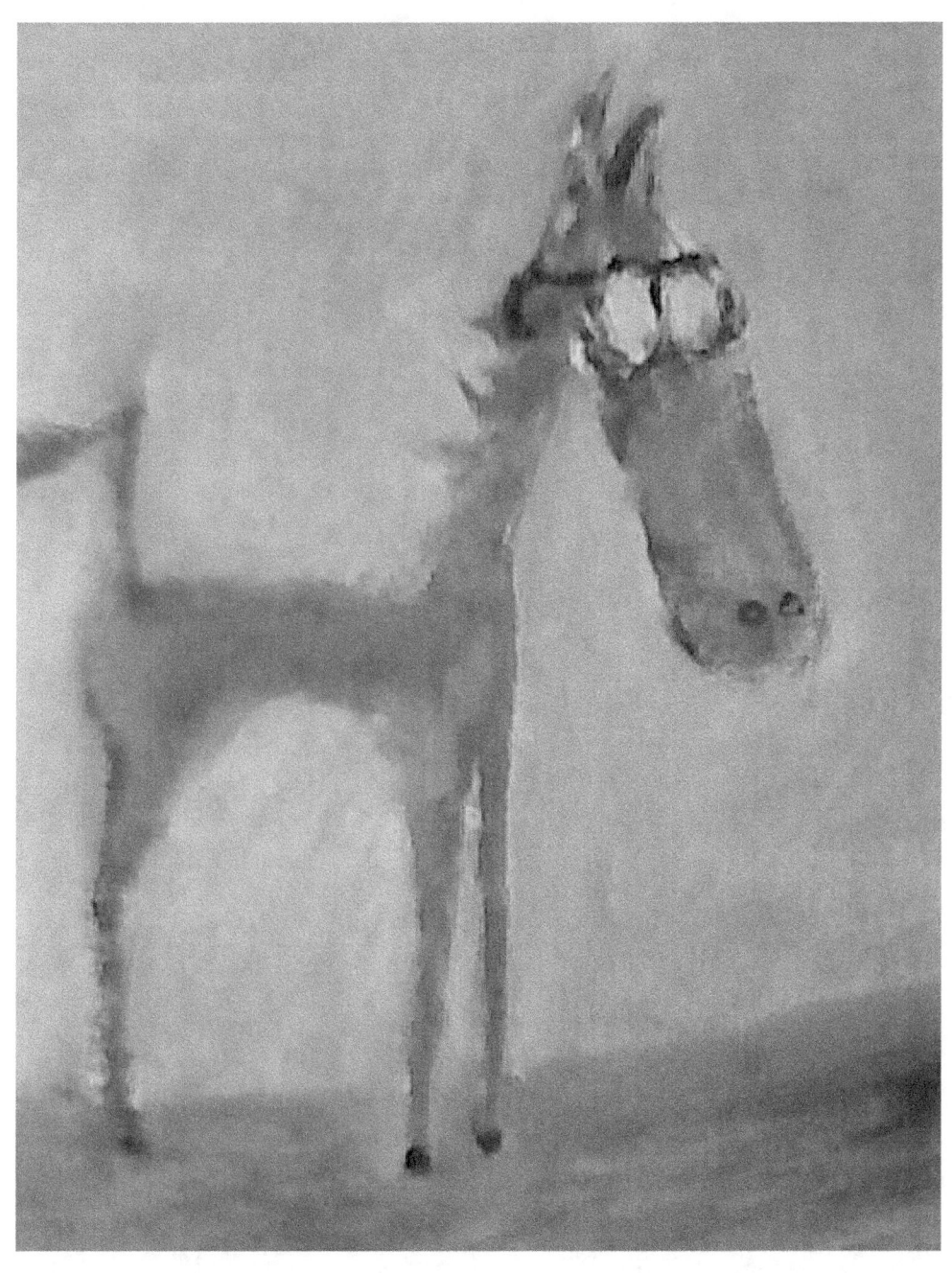

From "Seabiscuit" painting, showing horses waiting in line to see the movie.

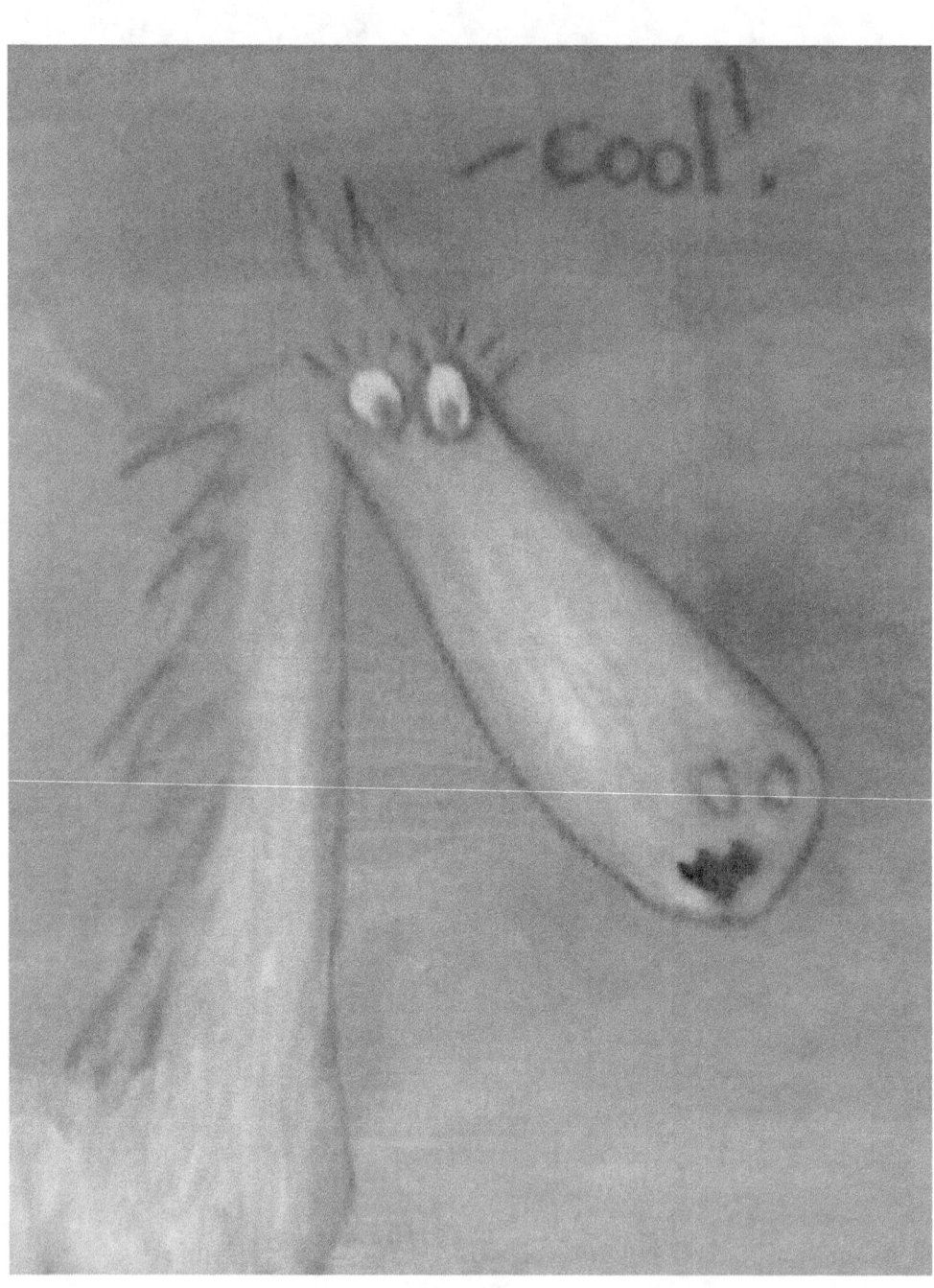

From "Saratoga Writers Group" painting—the horses are gathered around a table on which is placed the book, "Seabiscuit."

You can go to Cooperstown

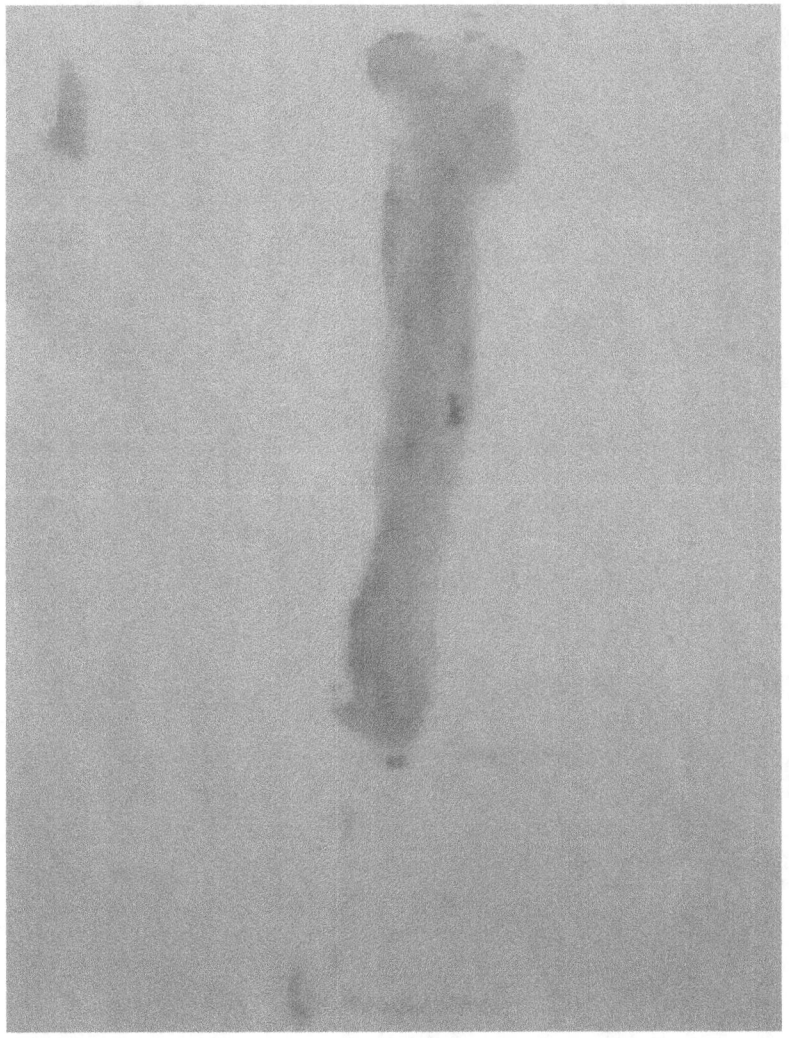

Otsego Lake

or Nelliston, a fine village

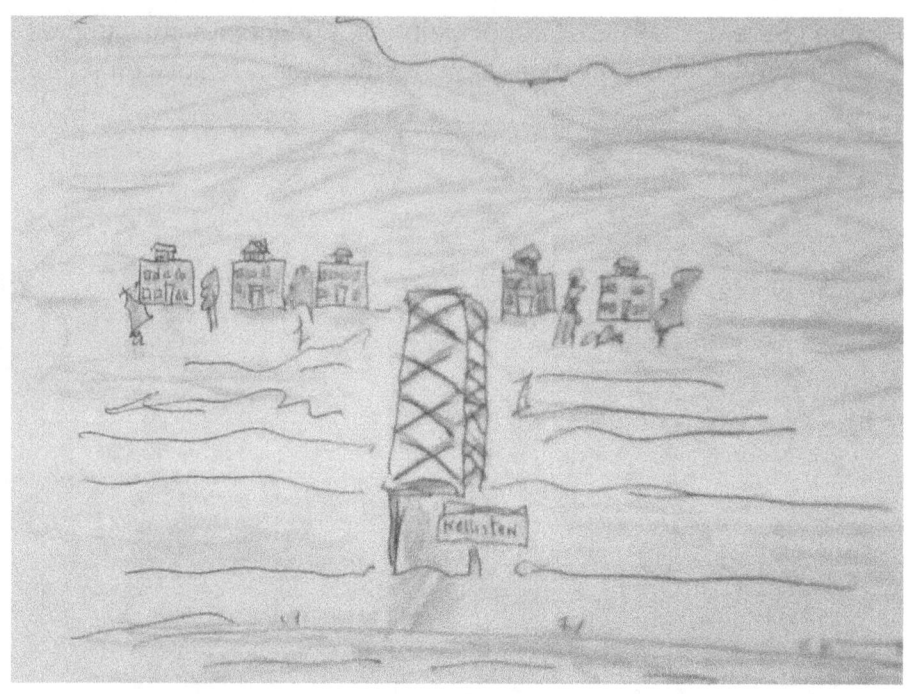

perhaps see a play in the Trojan Hotel

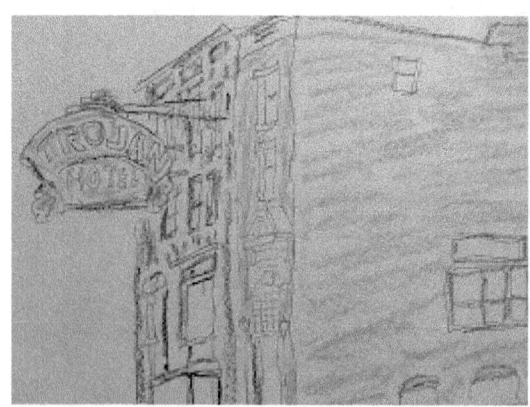

Trojan Hotel

beautiful Frear Park in Troy

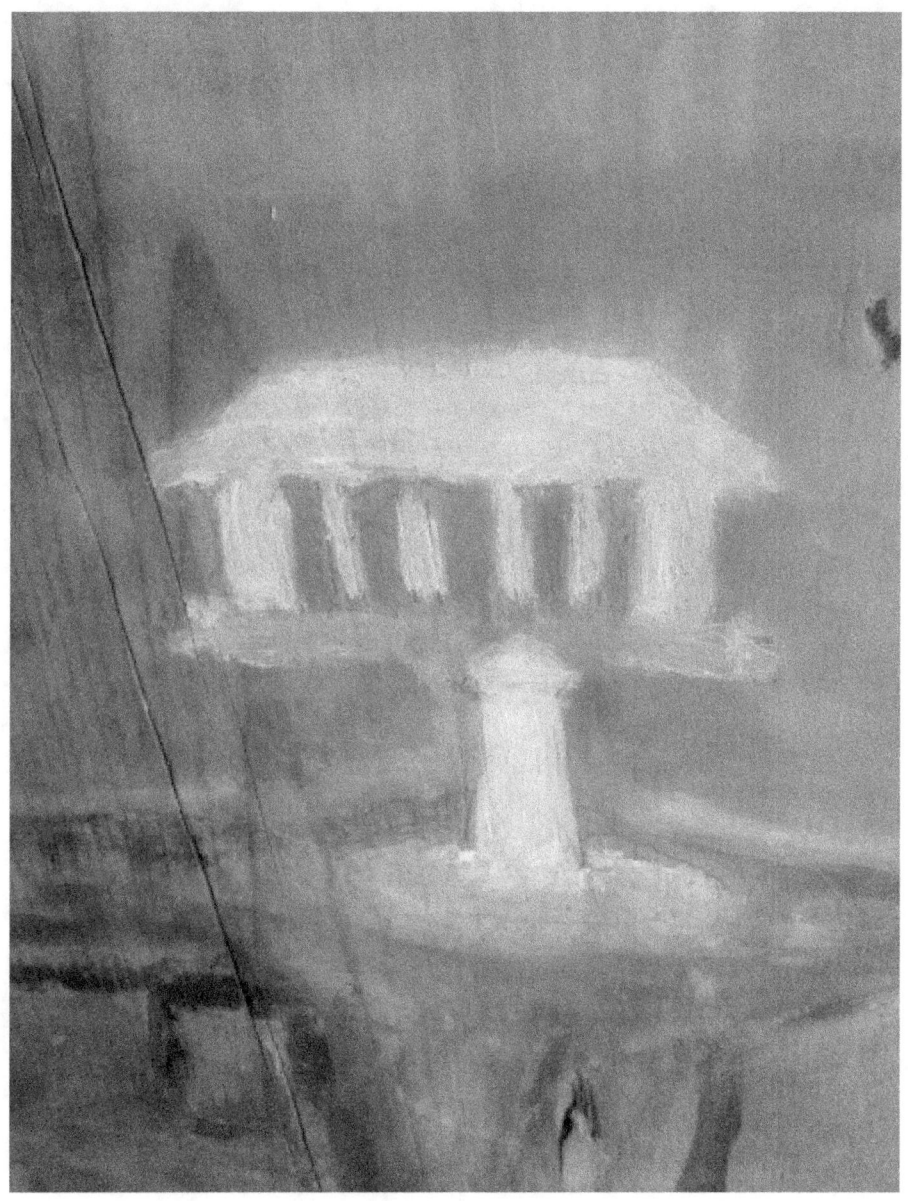

Frear Park Wedding Chapel

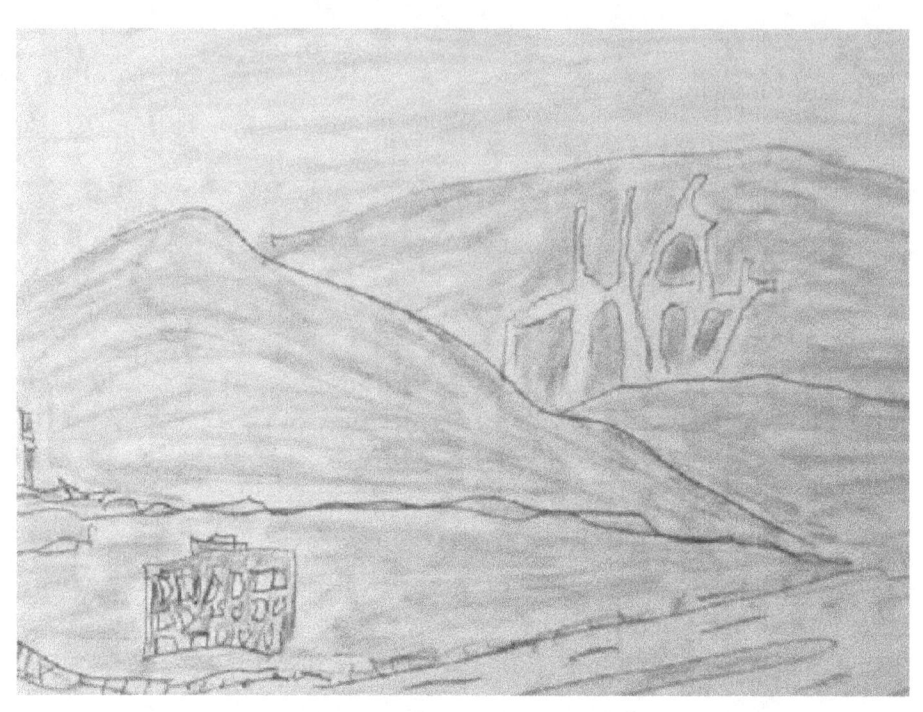

the end, for now

Book Two

Art and Limericks

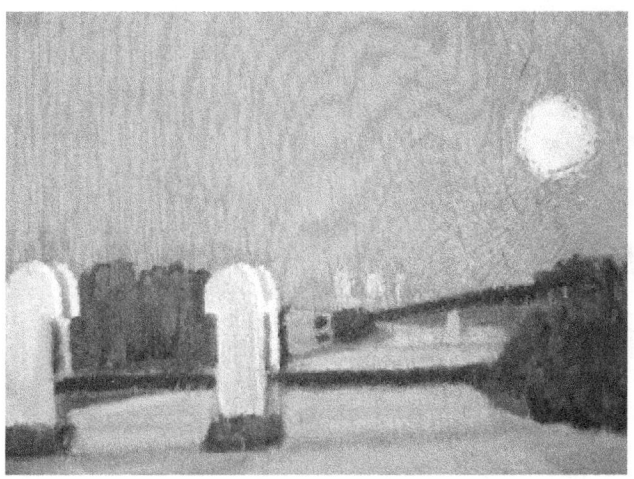

Troy

Thrills

When I was just a boy

I wanted nothing but a toy

Then I met a girl

who gave my heart an incredible thrill.

And where did I meet her?

Troy.

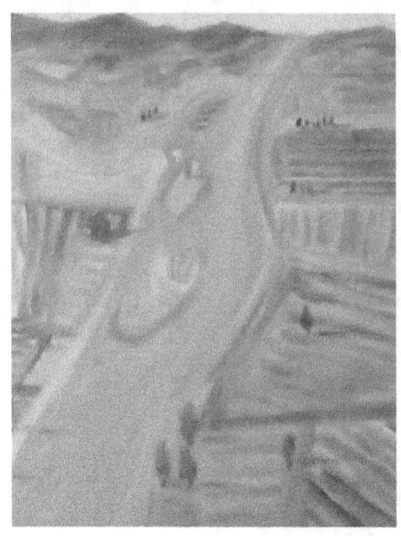

TroCoWaWaMeGi

Helen of Troy

I read a book called the Iliad

about a guy with an ego and an id.

To Troy he brought a horse

and a stunning Greek force.

All for a girl named Helen,

I do not kid.

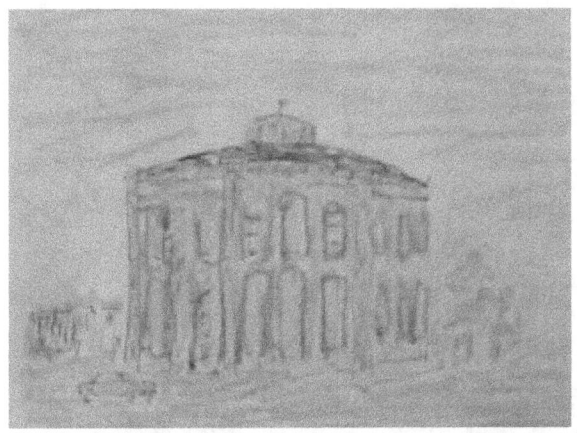
Gasholder House

Tomboy

I once knew a young man from Troy,

the city in New York filled with joy.

They asked him to go to Hanoi.

He said, don't draft me, I'll sign up,

and pretty soon he'd lost eighty pounds.

But he met a girl in Saigon who was a real tomboy

and now they write about their children like Tolstoy.

intermission

You can go to Cooperstown

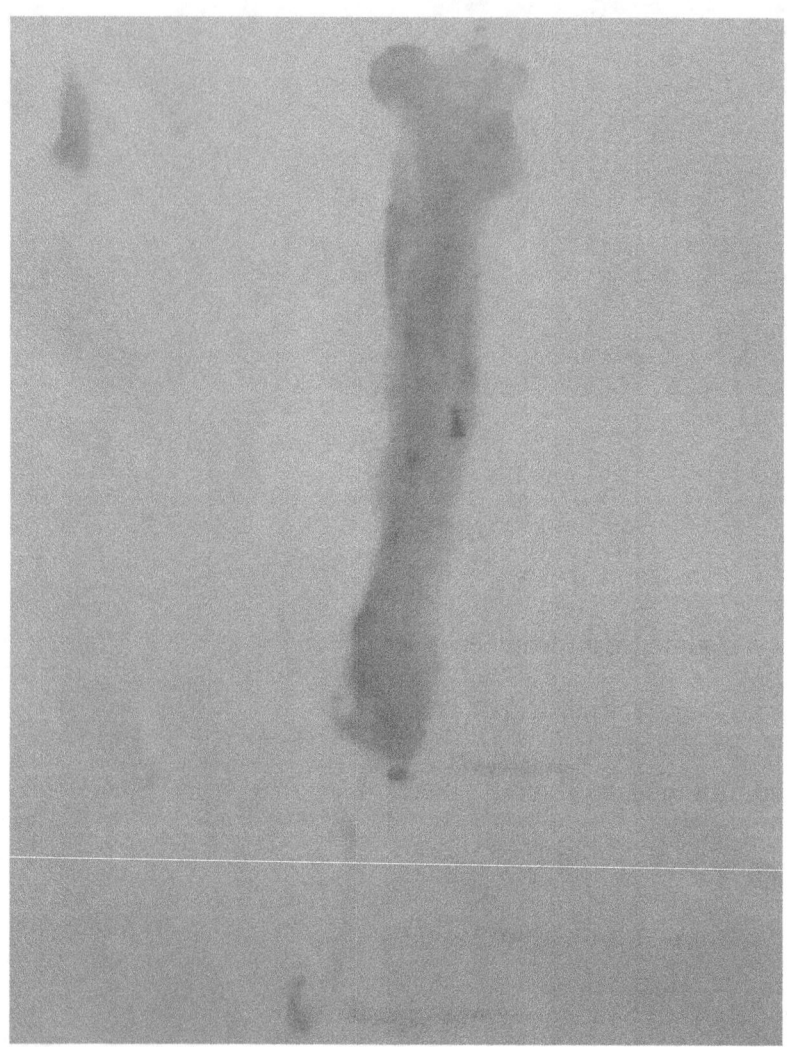

Otsego Lake

or Nelliston, a fine village

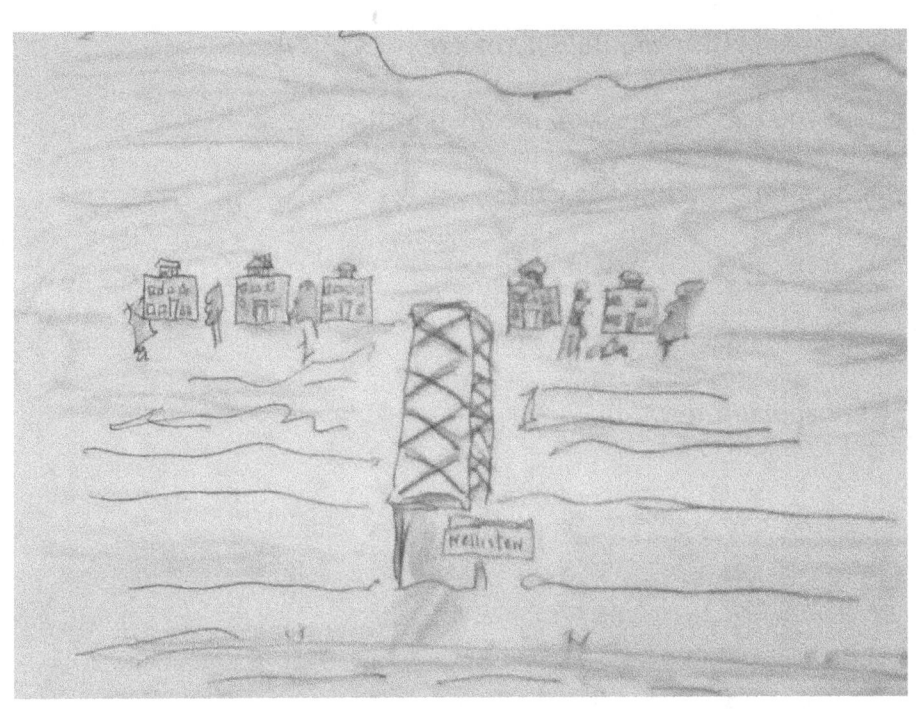

perhaps see a play in the Trojan Hotel

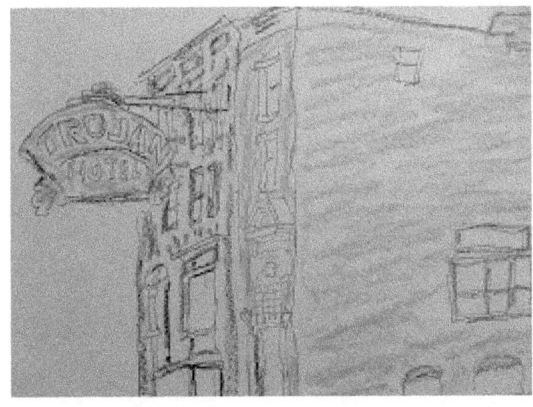

Trojan Hotel

Ahoy

I was born in the beautiful city of Troy

where you can hear girls on the boats yell, ahoy!

But then I moved to Cape Cod

until it became worse than jihad

so now I'm back in my hometown,

please applaud.

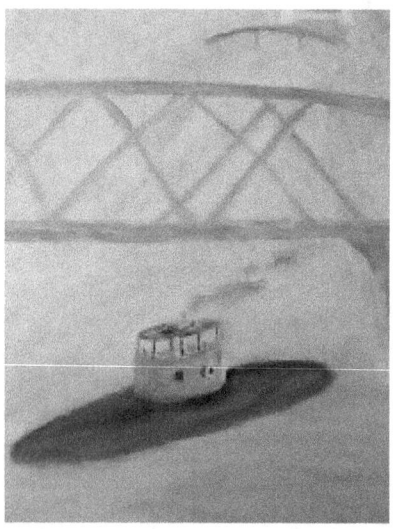

The Monitor

Buoys and Grrrls

At a grill in Troy she asked for a cigarette.

I said, I'm not that kind of guy.

She said, listen, you bellboy,

I just wanted a smoke.

Why don't you jump in the Hudson

and talk to a buoy.

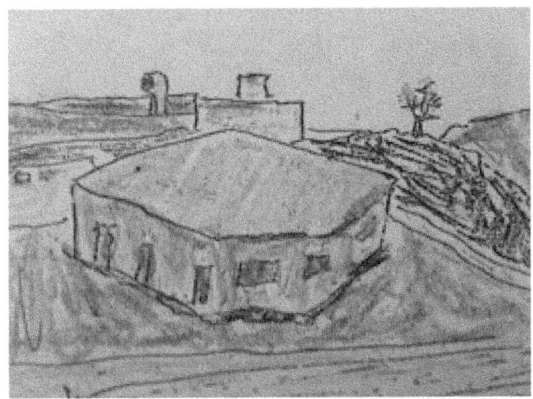

Roundhouse

Whipsawed

At the end of my fingers I gnawed

since I was being brutally whipsawed.

"Don't transfer me from Troy,"

I said. "I'm the best you employ."

"Don't worry, he said.

"We're sending you to Albany to destroy."

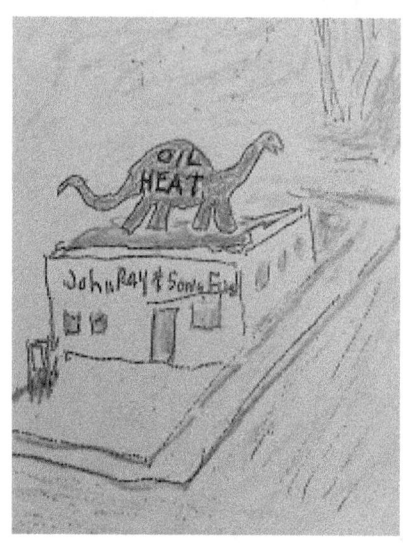

Ray's Dinosaur

Blurry

There was a guy from Troy

who said he'd like to go somewhere sandy.

So, Uncle Sam sent him to Nam.

"How could the U.S. be so unfriendly?"

he said. "My eyes must be blurry

and my brain a bit furry

but if you ask me, this place isn't surfy."

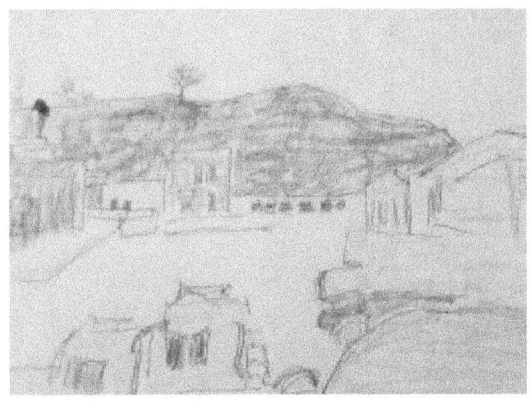

Mount Olympus

Barges

There was once a young lad

from a Hudson River city

where tugboats and barges used to play.

But then they were gone, and he was sad

so he set off to find fortune

in Lake Tahoe, Surf City and Tampa

but soon realized

there are no sinkholes in Sycaway

or volcanoes in Albia,

tornados or hurricanes in the Burgh

and no earthquakes or forest fires in Beman Park.

He said, "I'm going' home!"

You can take the boy out of Troy,

but you can't take Troy out of the boy.

Last Intermission

visit an abandoned ski area near Little Falls

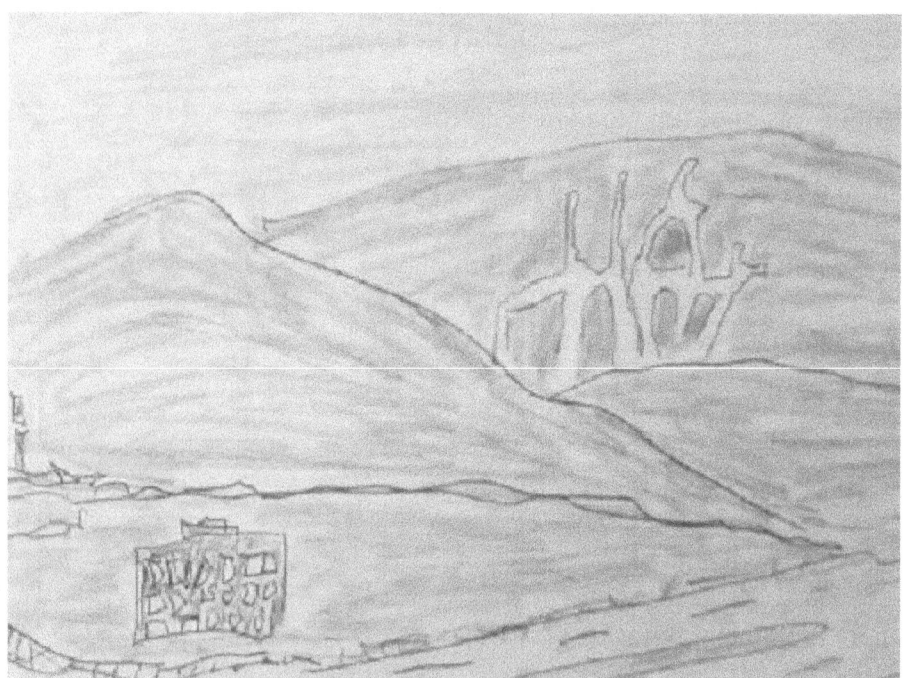

Shumaker Mountain

many artists exhibited their art near the canal in Little Falls, NY

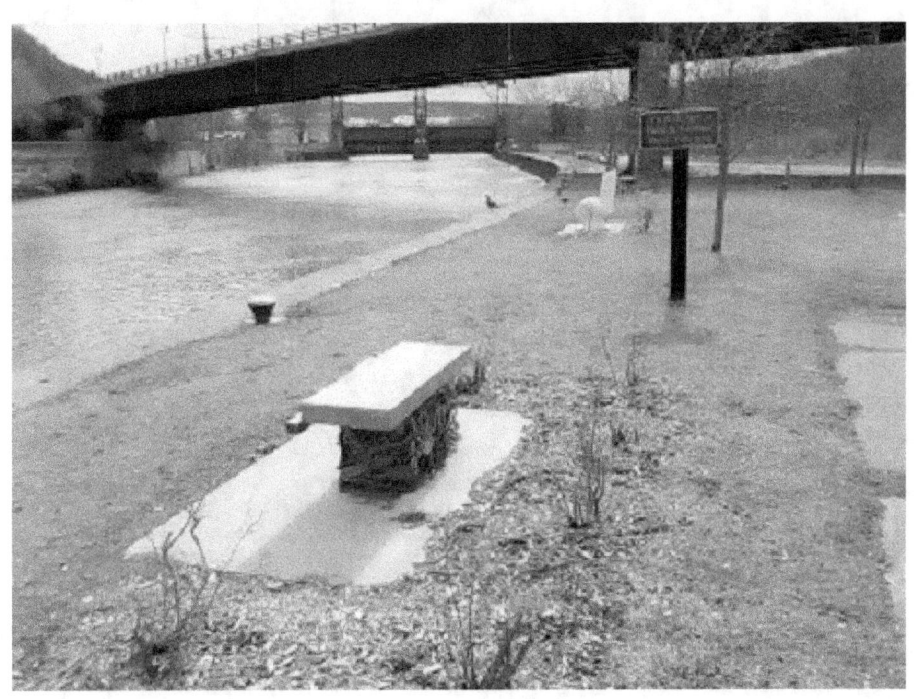

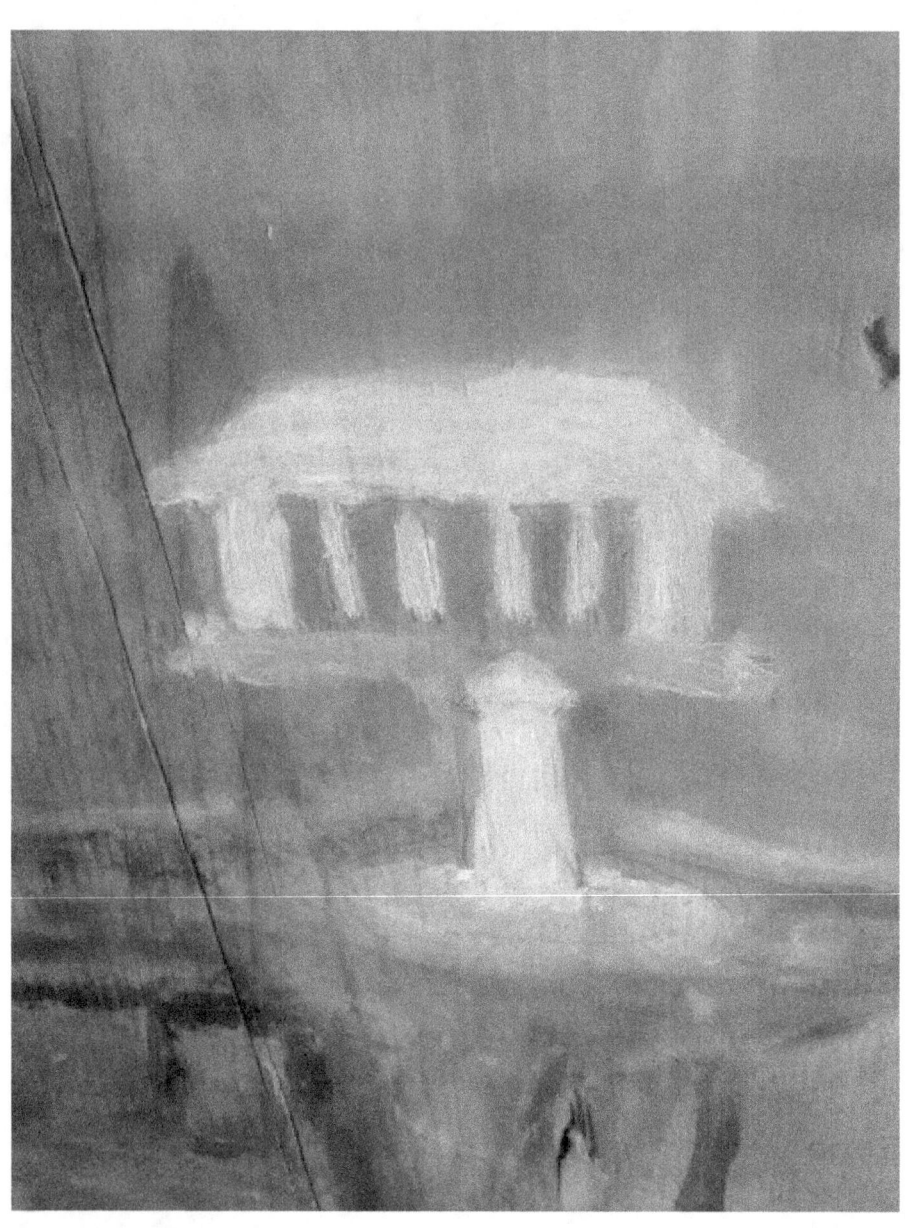

Frear Park Wedding Chapel in Troy, NY

Book Three

Art eBook

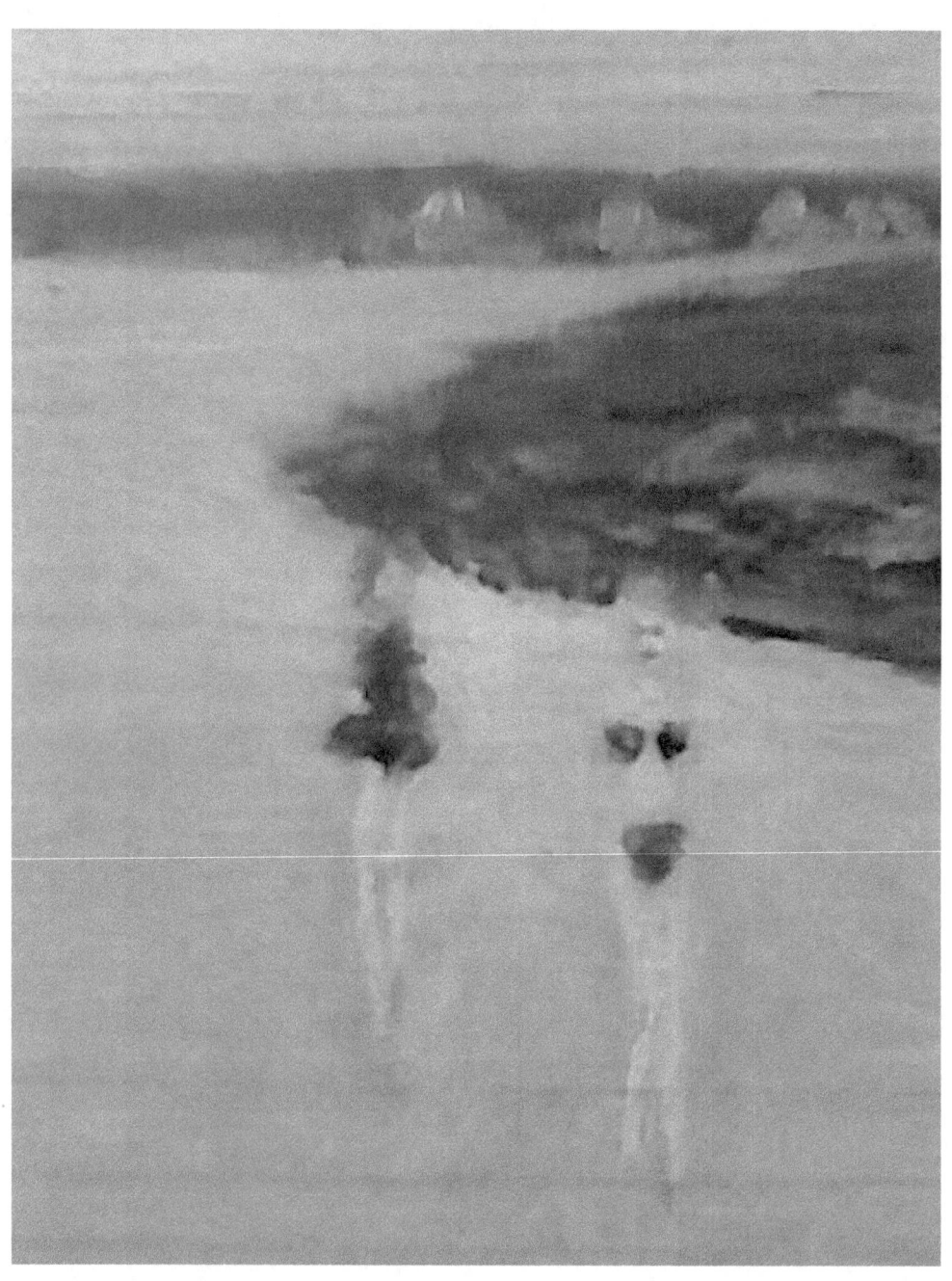

Craigville Beach, Cape Cod

near Hyannisport, painted on location, *en plein*

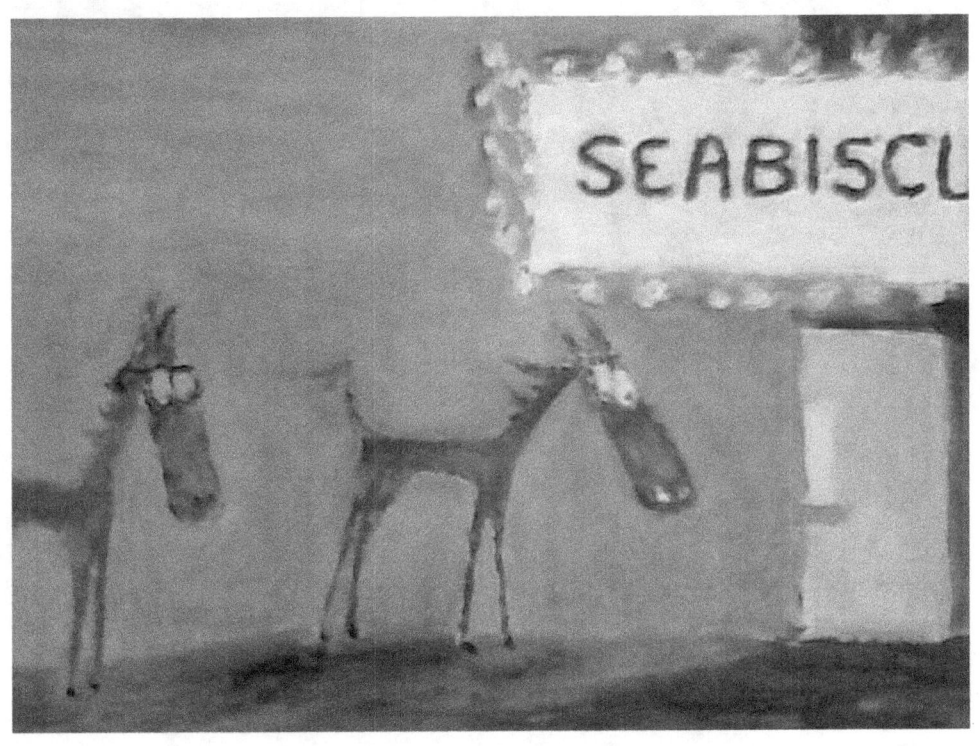

Seabiscuit

Horses attend movie theatre showing of "Seabiscuit."

Blandly was inspired by his brother-in-law, Michael David Smith, getting a role in the film "Seabicuit."

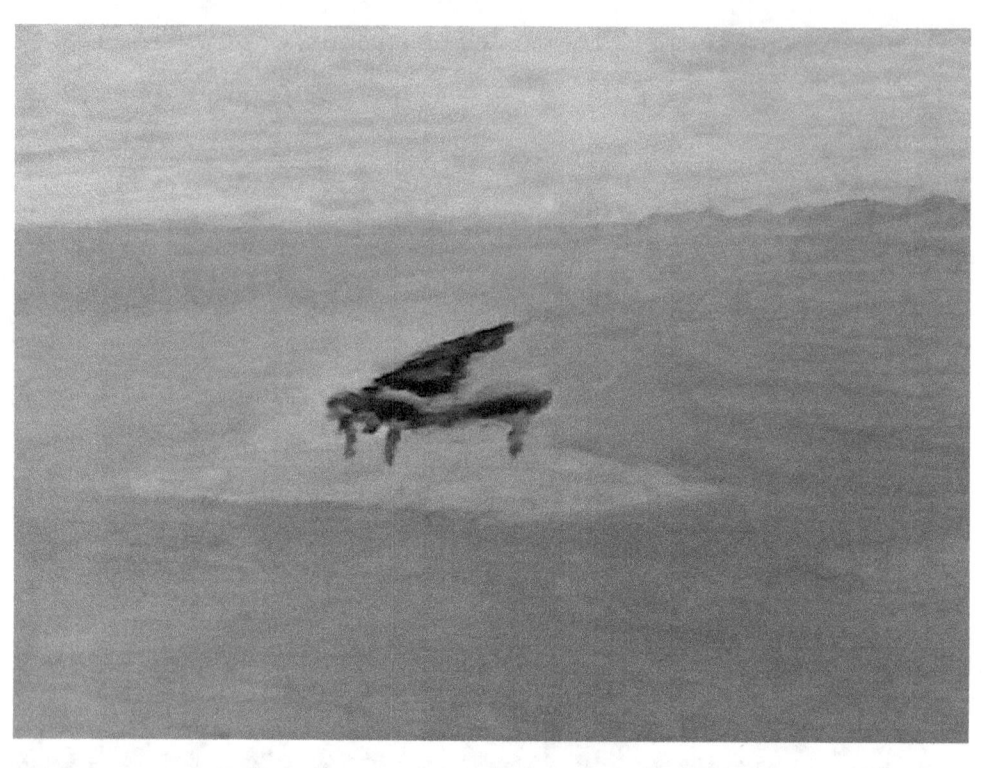

Biscayne Bay Sandbar Piano

Depicts a true story event, when a high school student, name unknown, managed to transport a baby grand piano to a spit of sand in the middle of Biscayne Bay, near Miami. Selected in 2013 for two art exhibitions, Fence Select, at the Arts Center of the Capital Region, in Troy, NY and the Mohawk-Hudson Regional, at the Hyde Museum in Glens Falls, NY.

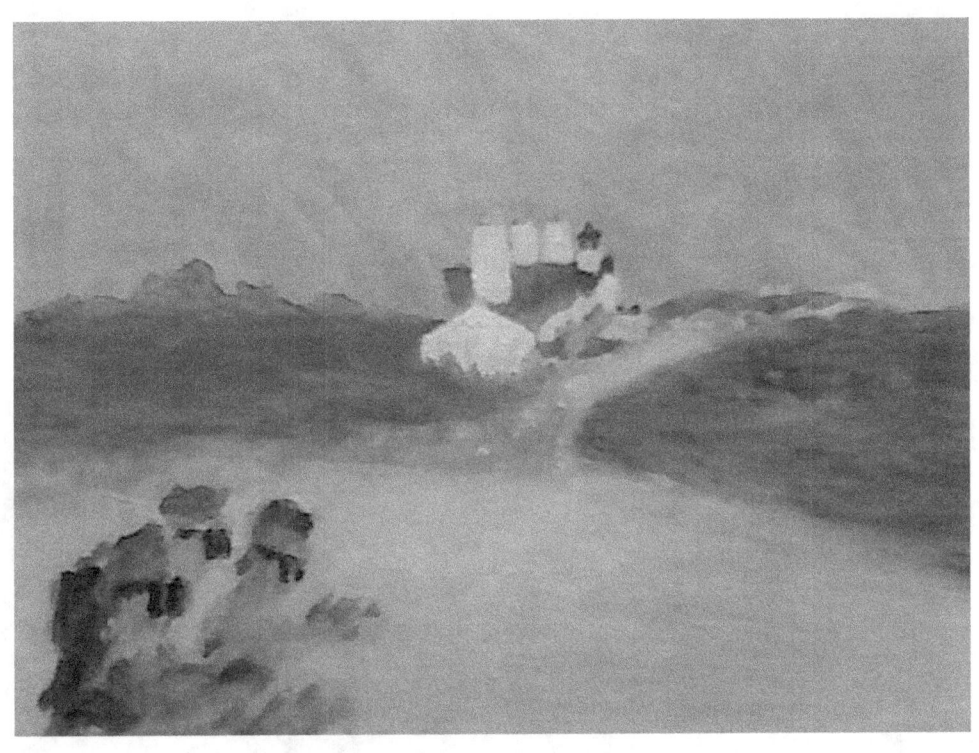

Sunglasses at West Dennis Beach, Cape Cod

Shows Lighthouse Inn in the background at West Dennis Beach.

Blandly shot a short film, "Young Lightman," guerrilla style, at the Lighthouse Inn. He toured the lighthouse there a year later, taking a trip up to the top inside the lighthouse, and sent a photo of the painting to the proprietors, and asked if they'd like to exhibit it there. They had other paintings on the walls of their bar and restaurant. The proprietors said no thanks. The painting depicts Blandly's beloved wife, son and daughter.

One of Blandly's films, featuring his wife, destined to ascend directly to heaven, the lovely, talented and long suffering Matilda Street, is "MShowBiz Awards." It is on YouTube.

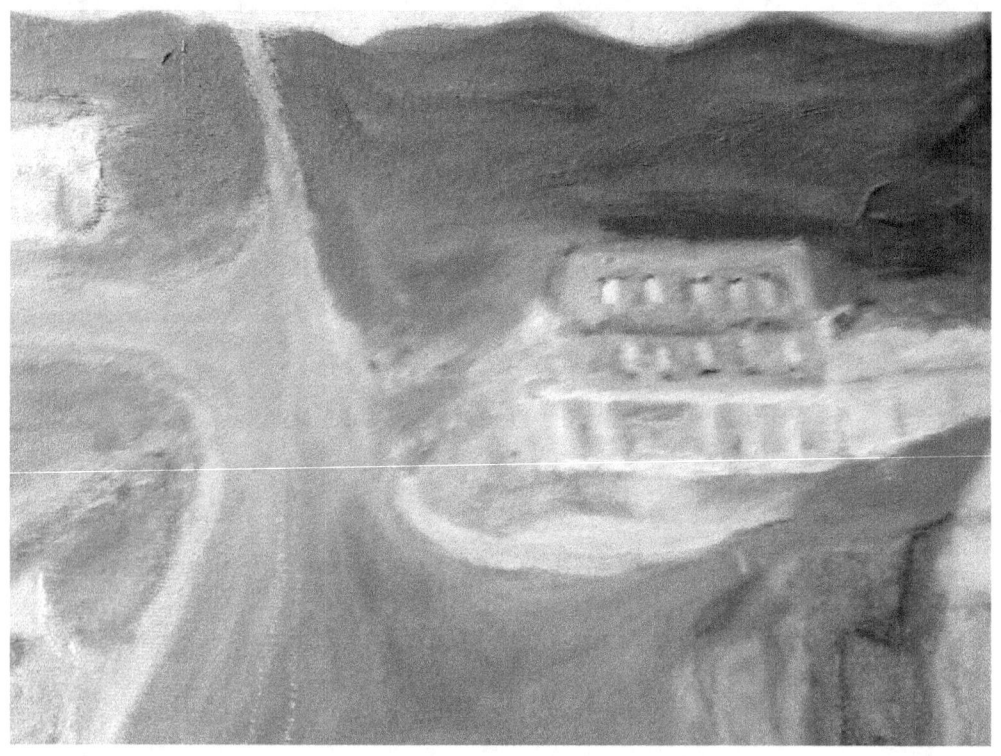

This small painting depicts the Northshire Bookstore in Manchester Center, Vt.: Blandly contacted the owners, asking them if they'd like to exhibit the painting, but they weren't interested.

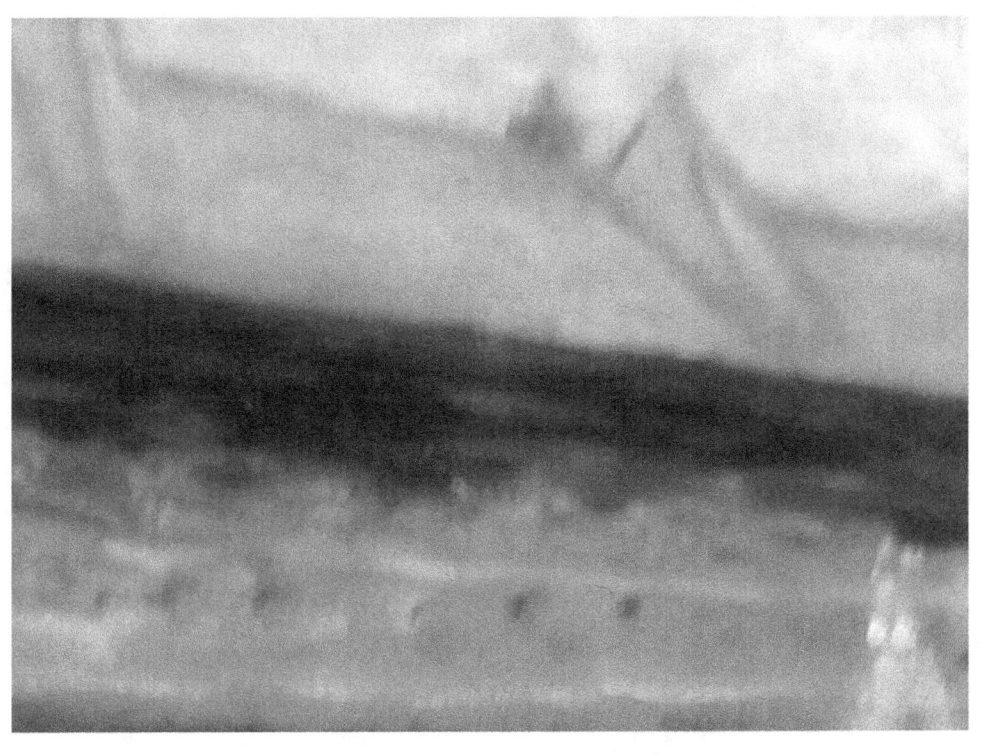

Ghost Horse #99

At the Saratoga Springs Art Center, a volunteer, taking in this paintings for a juried exhibition, said, "Wow, it's number 99." This was the number given to the painting by coincidence. It is a painting of Saratoga Race Track. Often white horses are called ghost horses—this one is an actual ghost—kind of like the one you bet on that never came in. It was selected for exhibition.

The photo is fuzzy. Sorry.

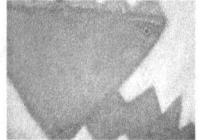

Lake Champlain Sea Monster

Painted at Basin Harbor Club, Lake Champlain, with the assistance of Blandly's sister, Christine Breitenfeld, who added lipstick and long eyelashes clearly showing "Champ," the Lake Champlain Sea Monster, is a female.

Circa 1990's, it was the first painting that Blandly attempted to exhibit, and was selected for Fence Select by an assistant curator from the Museum of Modern Art

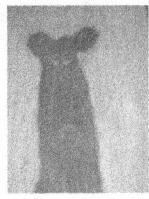

The Bear

Dimensions 1 ½' X 4 ½ '---a large oil painting on wood, "The Bear" appears on the back cover of the book, "The Greatest Novel Ever Written," as a photo of "the author."

Sold after an exhibition at the Spencertown Art Center, Spencertown, NY.

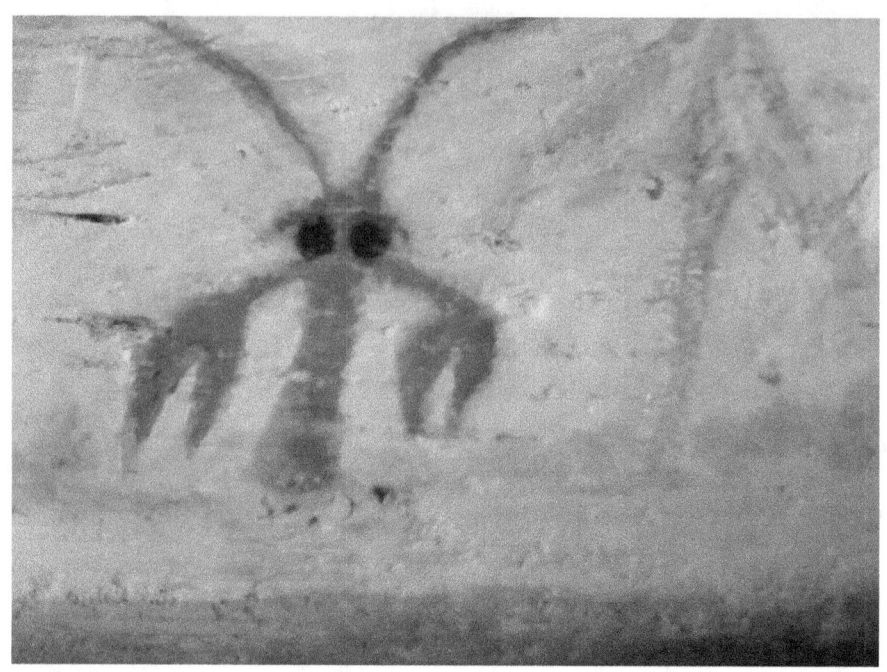

This painting, "Beach Lobster," was also sold at the Spencertown Art Center after an exhibition.

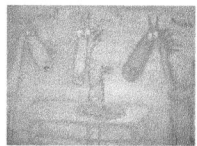

A very small photo of "Saratoga Writers Group." Blandly brought this painting to a session of his writers' group and had a photo taken of the group behind the painting. He cannot locate the photo.

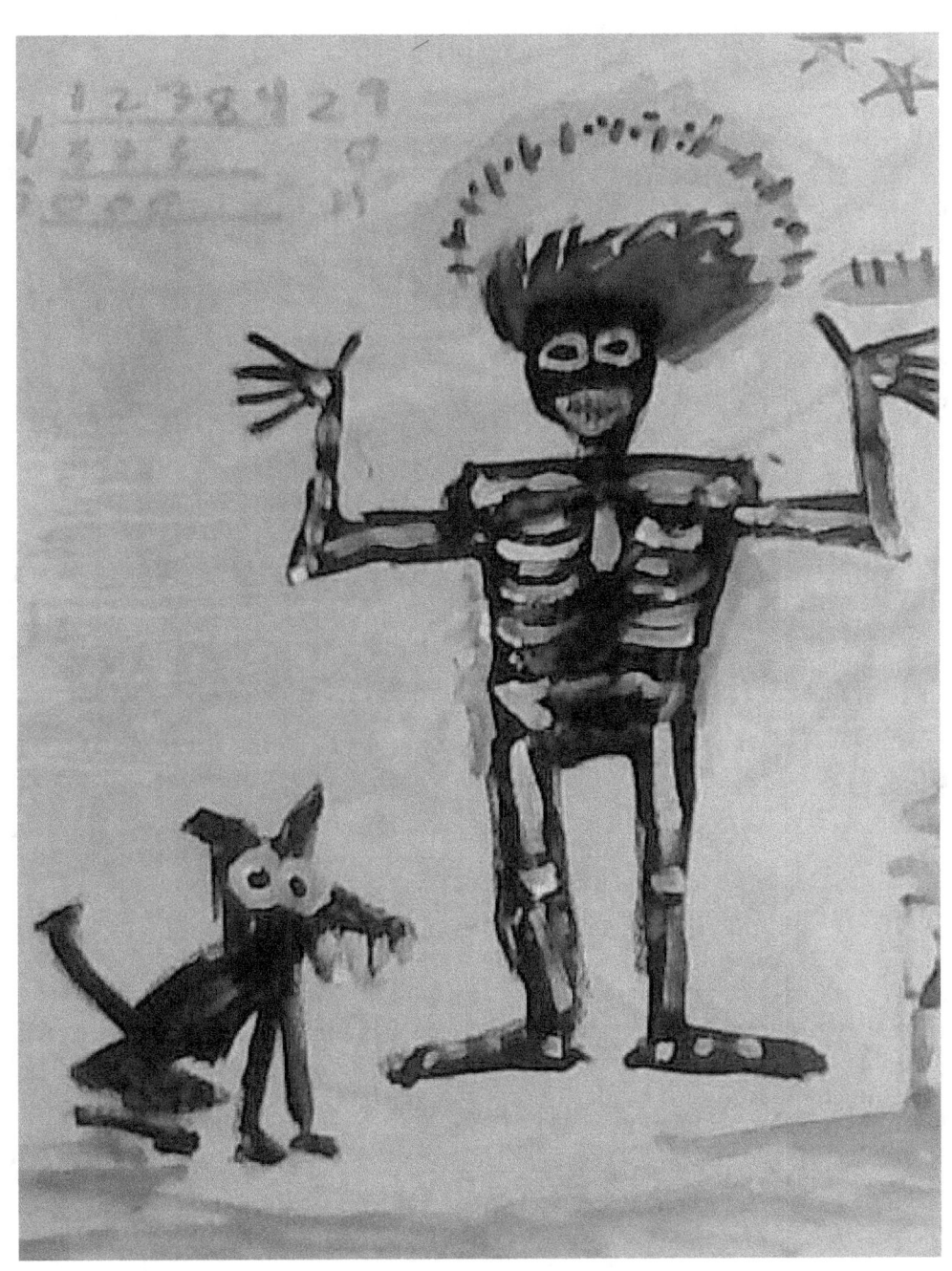

Self-Portrait as Basquait

In his style

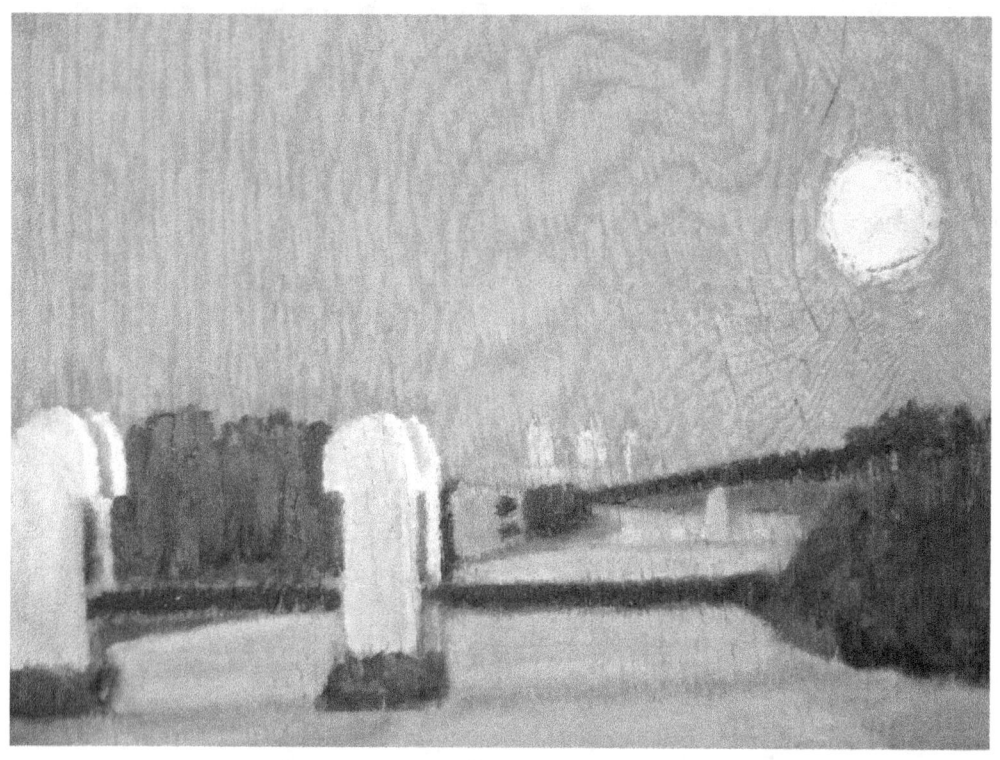

Troy

Fairly accurate oil painting, on wood, of Blandly's exciting and fantastic hometown. He has used it on zazzle t-shits, the only product he has ever sold there.

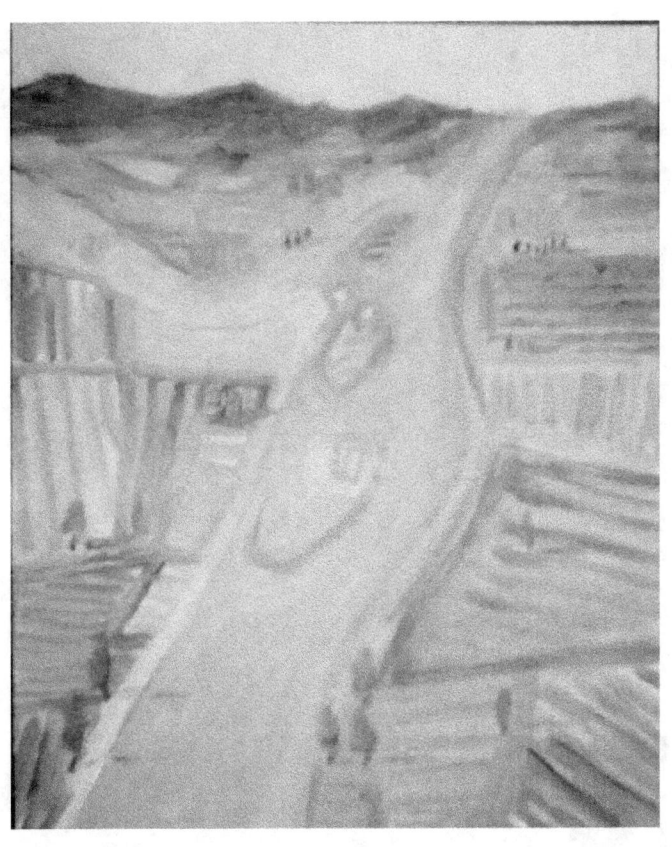

TroCoWaWaMeGi

A painting, Wayne Thiebald style, of the cities of Troy, Cohoes, Watervliet, Waterford, Menands, and Green Island, in upstate New York, a small metropolitan area with common interests, whose residents often attend the same high schools.

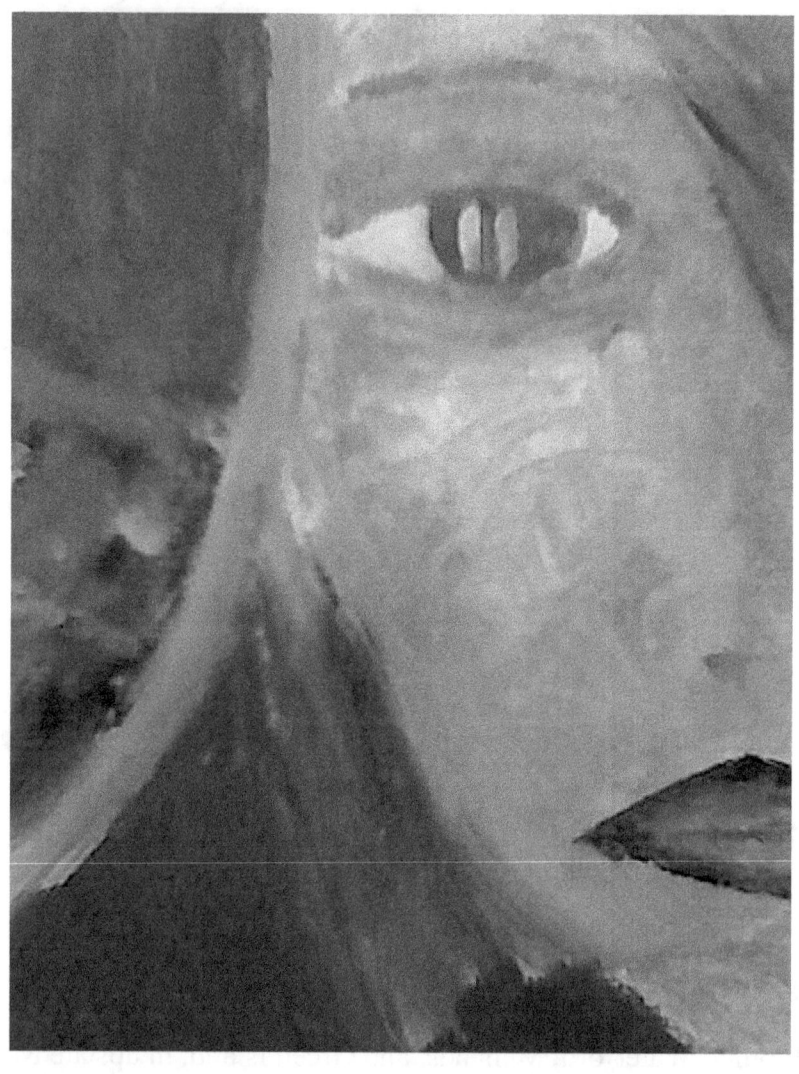

A small part of "Artgirl" based in part on a famous painting that depicts the World Trade Center Towers reflected in the girl's eye. The original painting was by Michael Perez, who painted a series of paintings he called "America the Beautiful."

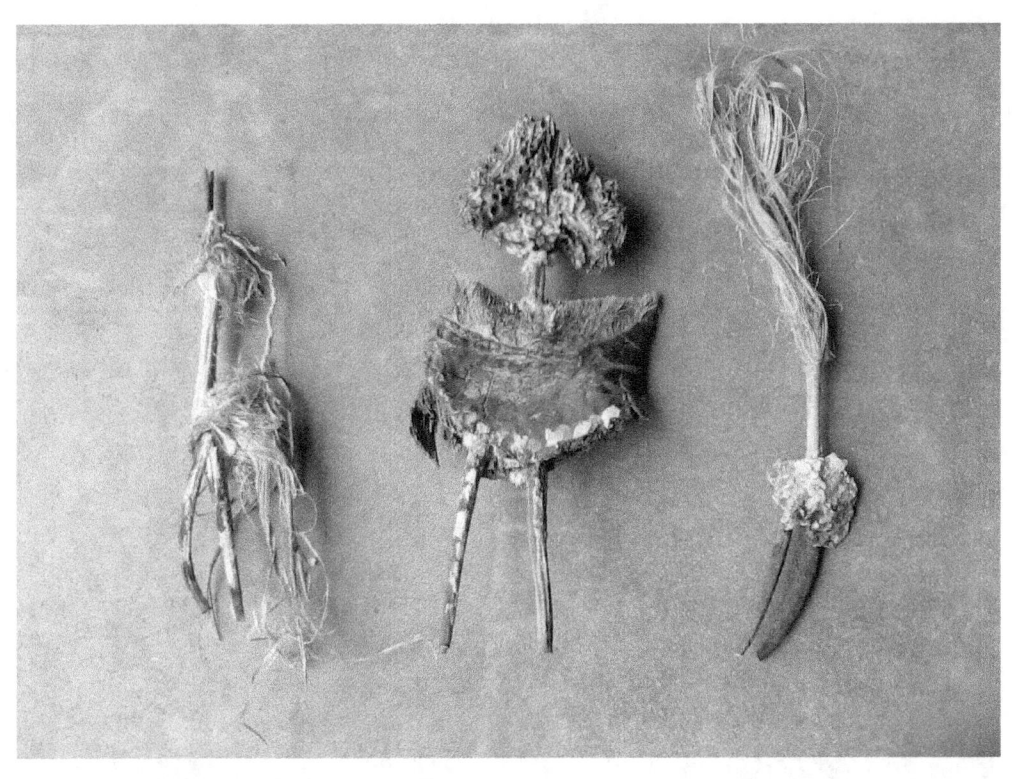

Marco Island Girls

A collection of painted driftwood—done on a beach at Marco Island, Fla. A day later, at a bar across the street from his hotel, a beachgoer congratulated Blandly for doing something so crazy.

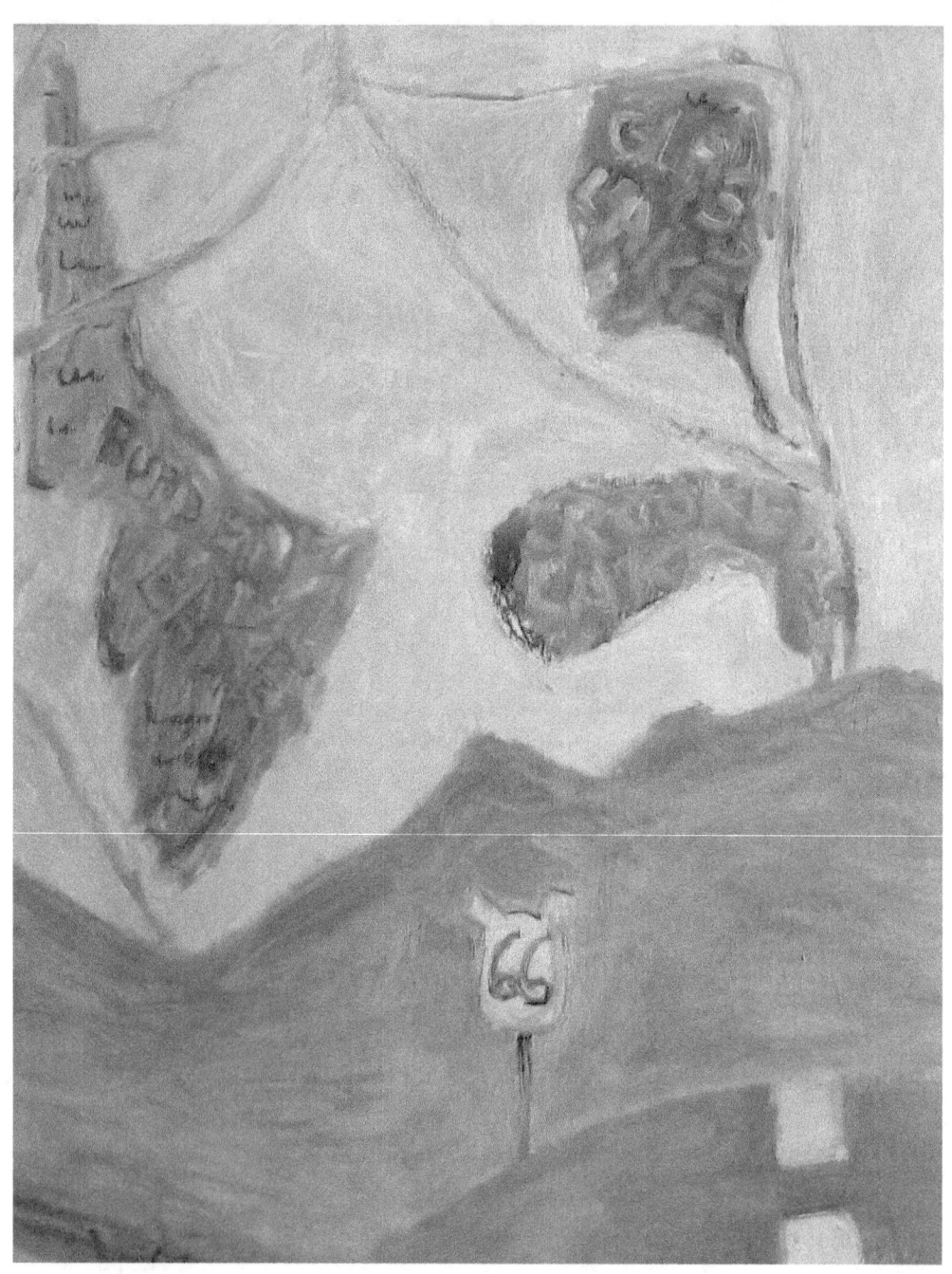

Rte 66

This is an attempt by Blandly to portray an area in Rensselaer County that includes Glass Lake, Crystal Lake, Burden Lake and Crooked Lake. These lakes are spectacularly beautiful. Blandly's grandfather lived on Glass Lake for many years. His great grandmother lived on Crooked Lake for a while. This photo shows only a portion of the painting, and is missing Crystal Lake.

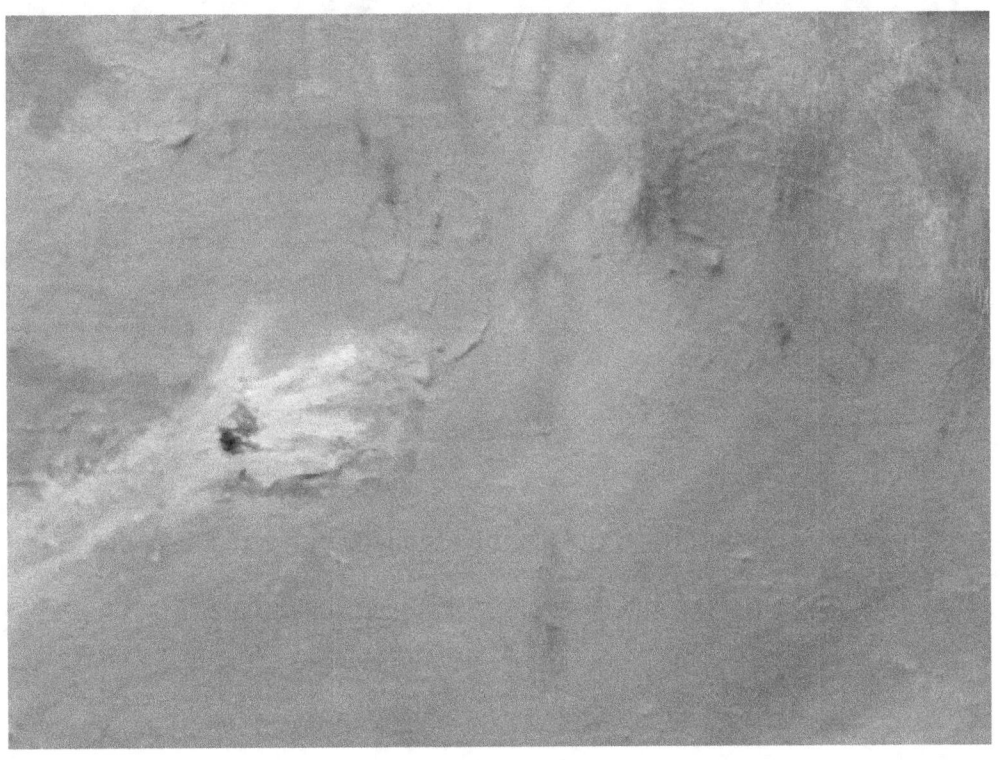

Hand on Cross

Now on exhibit at the St. Agnes Cemetery office in Menands, NY.
Or it was. It may be lost.

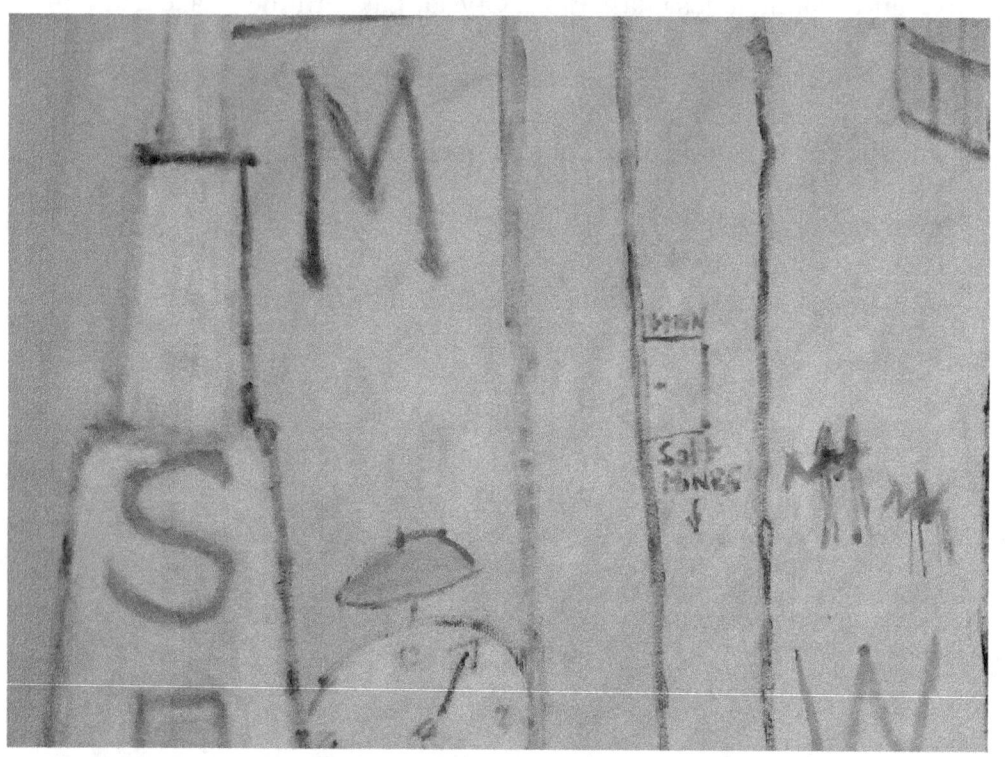

Ecumenical

This is a small portion of the painting, which depicts the days of the week, and the different sabbath days of three religions.

Other ebooks by John Blandly

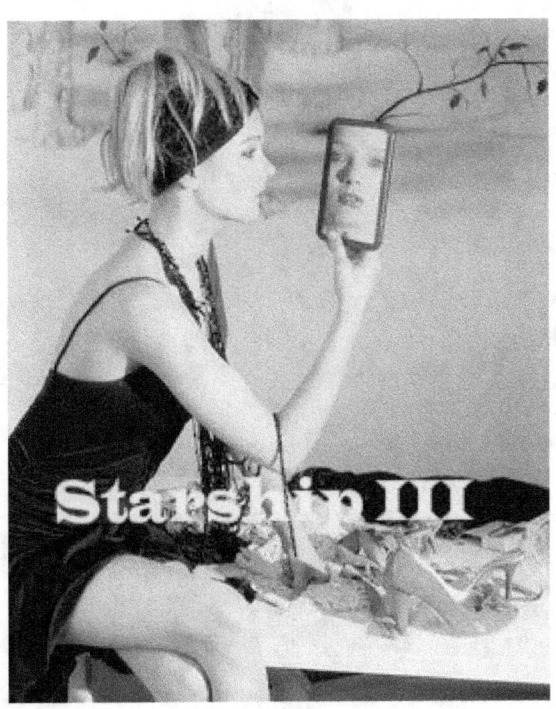

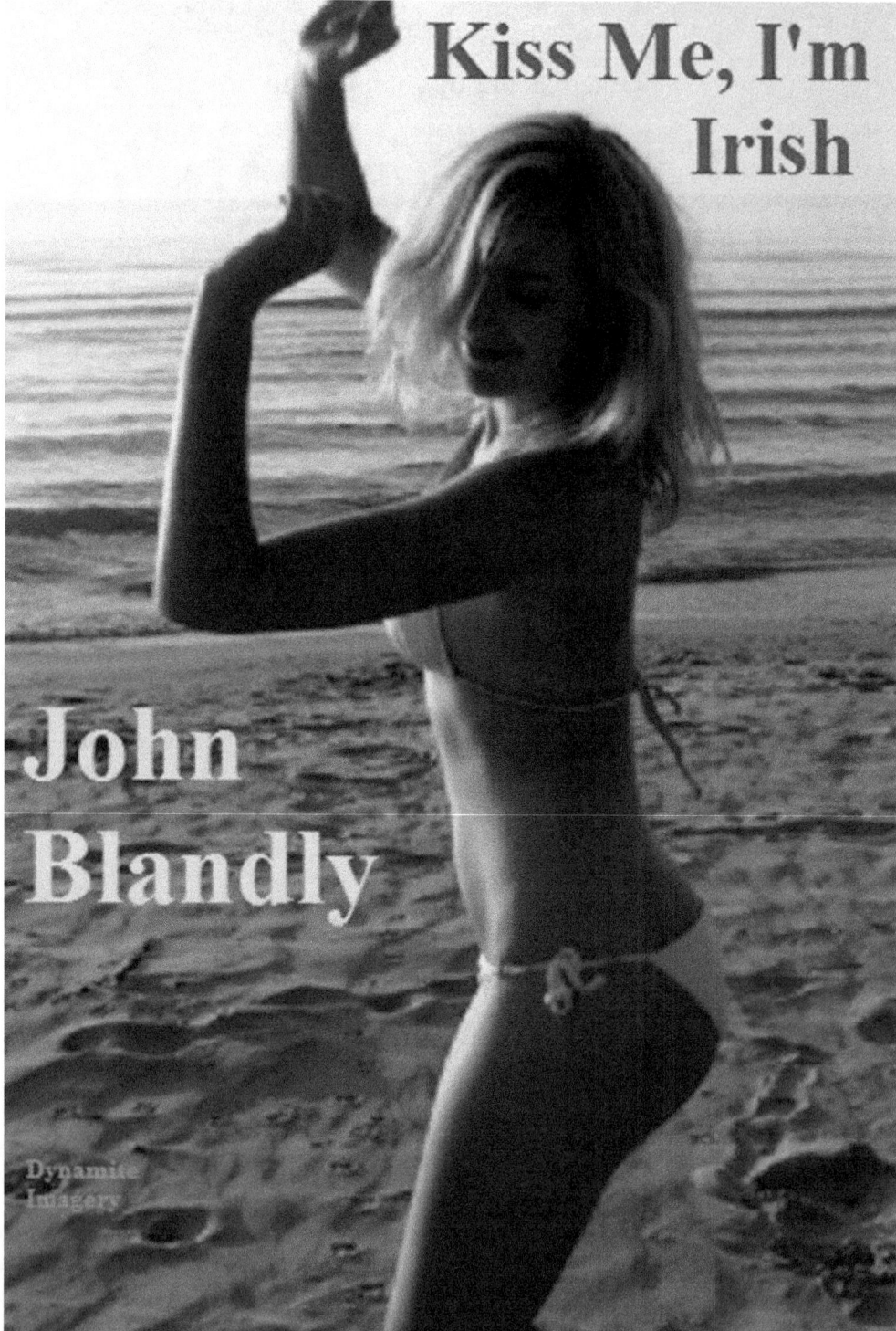

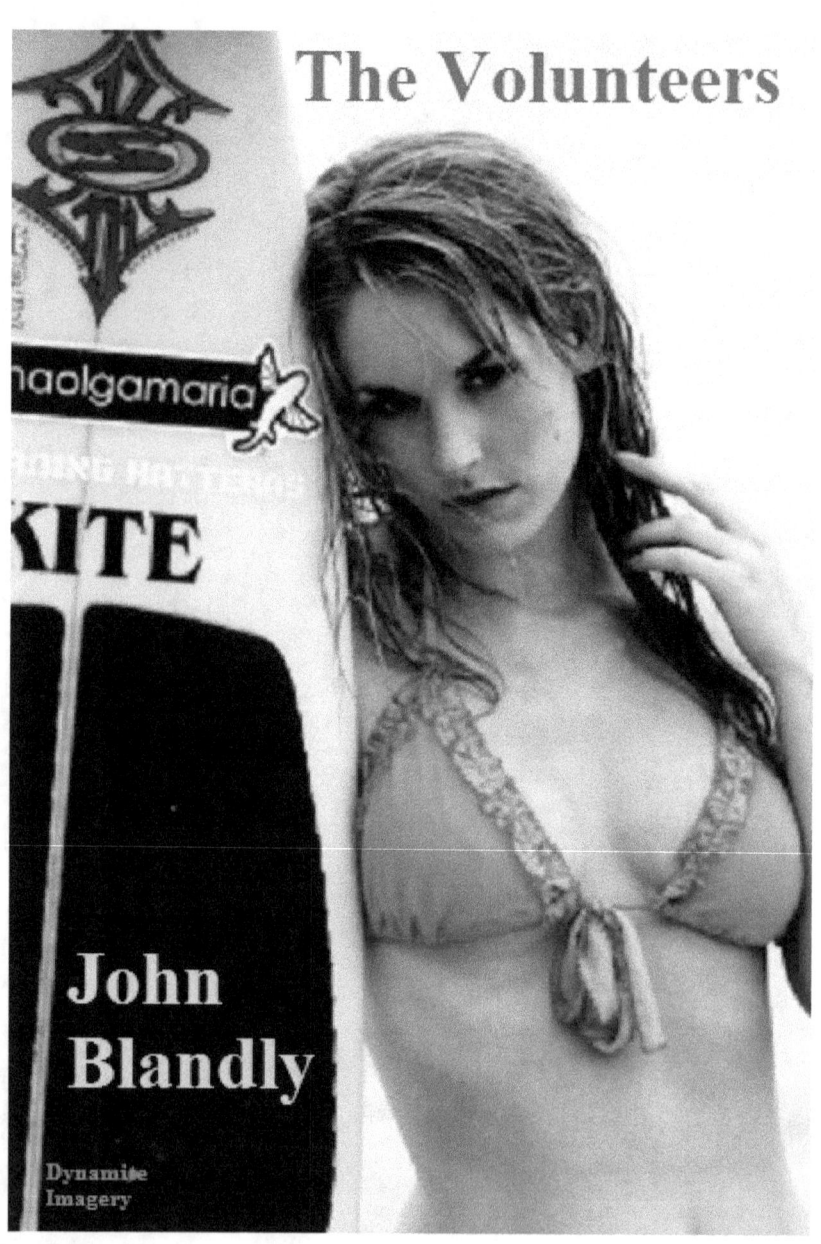

The end end

www.ingramcontent.com/pod-product-compliance
Lightning Source LLC
Chambersburg PA
CBHW050313220526
45465CB00005B/1964